GAME CHANGER

GAME CHANGER

An Aussie's Transformative US College Tennis Journey

Chris Bates

ILLAWONG BOOKS
BRISBANE

© copyright Chris Bates, 2020

This book is licensed for your personal enjoyment only. It is sold subject to the condition that it shall not, by way of trade or otherwise, be resold, hired out, or otherwise circulated without the author's prior consent. Thank you for respecting the hard work of this author.

I have tried to recreate events, locales and conversations from my memories of them. In order to maintain their anonymity in some instances I have changed the names of individuals and places, I may have changed some identifying characteristics and details such as physical properties, occupations and places of residence.

Please note all spelling is in English (Australia).

Book Cover Design by ebooklaunch.com

Contents

Foreword 1
Dedication 5
Praise for Game Changer 7

1. The Arrival 11
2. In the Beginning 33
3. Tennis Is Life 49
4. Getting Serious 69
5. The Rush 81
6. America 1.0 99
7. The Heart of the Matter 133
8. Home Again 145
9. Play Two - Back To College 153
10. America 3.0 - Making Things Right 183
11. The Team Comes First 195
12. Savouring the On - Court Moments 207
13. A Final College Reflection 223
14. May 2017 225

Author's Note 229

Acknowledgments 231
About the Author 235

FOREWORD

I first met Chris Bates about 30 years ago. I was an 11-year-old who'd fallen in love with the game of tennis, hitting balls for hours at a time against one end of my family home in outback Australia. And Chris was a super talented lefty, the number one player in the state for our age, and also my first-round opponent in my first ever state tournament in Brisbane. As I stood across the net from him during our match warm-up, I had little idea of the beating he was about to hand me. But little more than 30 minutes later my tournament was over having won less than a handful of points during my 6-0 6-0 loss and left to contemplate the 600 kilometre (400 mile) journey back to my hometown of Biloela.

Since that first meeting, I've been lucky enough to join paths with Chris often throughout my life due to our love of sport, learning, optimal development, and fun; from our junior tennis days spending most of our free time competing or hanging with friends at tennis centers around Australia, to our college years with Chris playing at Oklahoma State while I was at Pepperdine University in Malibu, California, to travelling together playing tournaments during our summer college breaks in the USA mid-west. During our post college lives our friendship has strengthened while working together on various projects.

Throughout the years, I've grown to respect Chris immensely as a guy with an unparalleled passion and skill for helping kids develop both on and off the court in his roles as a coach, teacher, and college guide. Reading Chris's reflections on his college journey brought back to life my own powerful memories of a simply joyous time in my life. His story, as well as being a terrific read, reinforced my view that there is no comparison to the US college pathway for families who value an opportunity for kids to become adults in an environment which balances development in sport, the classroom, and life, while having a great time doing it.

I have a lot to be thankful for, and among those things is the role that my US college experience played in my life. Knowing the person Chris is now, reading his book made it all the clearer that college was also crucial in making him the fantastic man he has become.

Dr. Anthony Ross

GAME CHANGER

Performance Psychologist
Founder of Mentally Tough Tennis

DEDICATION

To Grammy,

Whose pessimism and optimism were equally as endearing. You were there from the start of this journey, a key component in establishing my love of life, someone with whom to share life's ups and downs.

You'd see me off on every tennis adventure and welcome me home, each time, with a cheerful tear. This book fulfils my promise to you to document my story.

PRAISE FOR GAME CHANGER

"Chris Bates was your typical sports-mad Aussie backyard dreamer who achieved his goal of becoming the number 1 junior tennis player in this country in his age group.

Together with the triumph though, came a few other things.

The heavy weight of huge expectations.

Injury and adversity and everything that goes with it.

A rollercoaster ride to the other side of the world – a long way from family and friends.

Ultimately, the immense pressure to make it and make it quickly... or else be cast onto the sporting scrapheap never to be heard from again...

How he survived that journey and what he learnt in the process is the gold that emerges from his book *Game Changer*.

For any young aspiring athlete anywhere in the world, the parent or family of one... anybody really, who is interested in a story about the reality of sport, Chris' book is a must read.

I highly recommend it..."

Rupert McCall OAM
www.rupertmccall.com.au

***

"Reading 'Game Changer' is like going on a tennis and rites of passage journey. Chris's firsthand account of the pressures, the highs and lows and the lessons learned on this sporting ride are worth their weight in gold. It is also a guiding manual for those who want to challenge themselves in the phenomenal US College system as an athlete and a person. Highly recommended for athletes, parents and anyone who loves a sporting yarn."

Bill Jaede, father of two US College student athletes.

***

"If your family is considering the US college pathway, *Game Changer* is a must read personal account of the incredible opportunities that lie within the US college system, written by a guy with an unparalleled passion and skill for helping kids develop both on and off the sporting field."

Dr Anthony Ross, world leading Performance Psychologist

1

THE ARRIVAL

February 1997

"Dear Gram,

I made it here safely, as you would have heard, and am loving it! There's so much to get used to with new foods, driving on the wrong side of the road, and even the vocab is different! I can see why you and Grandad always loved America so much."

***

After thirteen hours to LA and a delayed connecting flight, some winter January snow greeted me at Will Rogers International Airport in Oklahoma City.

It was a tick before midnight. Waiting for me near the baggage carousel was Coach Wadley, dressed in well-coordinated black and orange tennis gear from top to bottom. He was just as I remembered him from a year earlier, when he came to watch me play in an individual event in Waco, Texas. He couldn't have been taller than five-foot-nine, but he possessed a towering persona and a belly to match.

With a large grin and a strong, warm handshake, Coach looked really pleased to see me which was more than a little comforting. 'How ya doin' my main man?'

'Great thanks, Coach. So glad to finally get here.'

We bundled into the biggest minibus I'd ever seen and headed for Stillwater, home of the Oklahoma State University Cowboys.

I will never forget the trip.

It was snowing, for starters. That was different. We were driving on the wrong side of the road. That was weird. At one point, as gentle sleet kissed the windscreen, a deer appeared through the headlights on the side of the road. That was a unique encounter for a city kid from Australia who had barely seen a kangaroo let alone other antler wielding wildlife. Strange machines, bobbing up and down like ostriches digging for sand, littered the flat landscape. I learnt from Coach they were oil wells, some dormant, some active. In the space of one day, I had come from surf, sand, high humidity, and searing heat to close deer encounters, oil wells, and snow. I really *was* a long way from home.

The other thing I remember from that hour-long road trip is that I did not say a word. Those that know me now would find that hard to believe. It's not like I had a choice though. Coach barely drew breath the whole time. He covered everything from politics, to music, to tennis, to his coaching philosophy.

Welcome to America. I loved it already.

As we pulled into Stillwater in the early hours of the morning, the campus was a ghost town. Unperturbed by lack of sleep, Coach would pull over to the side of the road, playing tour guide to his newest recruit. Blinking sleepily in the passenger seat beside, I smothered a yawn as Coach pointed out Stillwater's interesting landmarks.

'Over there, Chris, is Theta pond which is frozen over right now. It's pretty neat in the daylight. You'll walk right by it tomorrow when we get you measured up for all your new tennis gear. You can see over yonder the big football stadium which seats over 60,000. Behind that is Gallagher Iba Arena where y'all will access all of your massage and physical therapy, as much as you need.'

'Looking forward to seeing it all tomorrow, Coach,' smothering another yawn.

Partly, I just wanted to get to my new room and sleep. I knew that tomorrow I would be in a better position to absorb all of this new information and get my bearings around campus. But at the same time, I was buzzing about the idea of waking up to start my first full day in Stillwater, Oklahoma.

Straight faced and out of the side of his mouth, Coach delivered a few laugh-out-loud jokes that are best left out of a book. I imagined that I would have been probably his hundredth recruit to whom he had told those jokes.

The bus eventually came to a quiet halt just near the tennis courts. For a moment I thought Coach was going to put me through my paces on court. He was, after all, dressed appropriately!

There, out to the left of the bus, perched on one of the highest points on campus were the twin towers of Willham dormitory, my home for the next semester. The Georgian style, rectangular, reddish-brown brick buildings were reserved for female and male freshmen, in separate towers. It looked more like a hospital than a dormitory, but as I would later discover, was centrally located and more importantly walking distance to all my needs.

'Ok, we've roomed you with Pavel, our new recruit from the Czech Republic. Y'all are up on the sixth floor. Let's go and get y'all settled in.'

I felt bad arriving so late and waking my new roomie. So, when he greeted me at the door, I was particularly quiet. I needn't have worried; Pavel was a friendly bloke despite his intimidating, pale, skinny frame that towered over me. On the surface we really couldn't have been more different. Pavel looked like his skin had never seen a summer. His short, thick, sandy-coloured hair was in stark contrast to my longer, thinning, curly, brown hair. Pavel looked more like a man than this wiry kid from down under.

'Hello,' he said in broken English.

'How ya goin' mate?' I asked, without a thought that maybe my raw Australian tone might have made my greeting difficult to understand.

'Good,' Pavel offered back with a slight shrug.

Coach then signed off for the night. 'Well alright, y'all seem fine together. Chris, I'll pick you up at 8am – big today tomorrow. Take this card and swipe it for your breakfast in the dining hall just to the left as you get out of the lift. It opens at 6am.'

A small night-light above Pavel's bedhead lit up the room enough for me to find my way to my bed. I lay in the same clothes in which I had left Australia some thirty hours earlier. As I drifted in and out of la-la-land, I couldn't help but notice Pavel's feet hanging over the end of his bed by a considerable margin. He was busy reading the Czech-English translation dictionary. I wondered if he was looking for ideas for conversation with his new roommate.

'Night mate,' I mumbled.

'Goodbye,' Pavel shot back in a deep monotone.

I chuckled to myself and then hit the pillow hard.

***

My first full day was upon me quickly due to the late arrival, and I didn't get nearly enough sleep. I think I signed my name about forty-seven times that day. I wasn't yet cleared to compete by the governing body of collegiate sport, the National Collegiate Athletics Association (NCAA). I needed to finalise paperwork, as well as enrol in classes, and get my student ID.

That was an experience. My photo was not flattering. I had been holidaying on the Gold Coast in Australia at the height of a hot summer with my family only thirty-six hours earlier. I had a beetroot-red nose and my whole face had that familiar peeling that is so identifiable for Aussies, especially those on the Gold Coast. But peeling in winter probably meant I was a frost bite victim. The photographers looked at me with pity, like I had just returned from an Antarctic mission. I was stuck with that ID for four years, a constant reminder to wear sunscreen at all times.

I met so many new people that first day, knowing I was going to have to ask them again for their names at a later date. I was given so much gear I didn't know what to do with it. Nike from head to toe. All had been embroidered with the Oklahoma State University logo, the letters OSU in the form of a cattle brand. Socks, t-shirts, polo shirts, shoes, tracksuit, vests, hoodies, even my tennis bag had the OSU brand and a combination of black, white, or orange, the colours I would come to love so much.

I took a whole film's worth of photos on my disposable camera that I had purchased days earlier at Brisbane airport and couldn't wait to tell my brothers back home about all of this free stuff under which I was almost buried. I was given my food-plan card, a card I could swipe for buffet breakfast, lunch, and dinner, anywhere on campus. This is what a full scholarship opportunity looked like. It was simply like nothing I had ever seen back in Australia. Nothing to this value was free.

Welcome to America.

Then came my teammates. Coach took me to the 'Aussie' house, a dated and rather ugly brown weatherboard townhouse, nestled right next to campus on Monroe St. There lived three of my teammates, Daniel, Brad, and Rob; all well and truly established college student-athletes. All Aussies. Daniel answered the door.

'Hey Coach. Hey Batesy! Come in mate,' he urged, stepping back with a sweep of his arm.

'Good to meet you boys!' I replied with a broad grin.

In I went, careful not to trip on the Sherrin football, various tennis balls, dirty, sweat-ridden gear, and reels of tennis string. The place was a pigsty! The messy room was flanked by two long, black, well-worn leather couches which looked like they had been handed down from generations of former Oklahoma State University tennis teams. What stories these walls and couches could tell.

Inside that front room with four Australians I could have been forgiven for feeling completely disoriented. With an oversized Australian flag featured on the main wall, the Australian Open tennis blaring through the TV screen, and three shirtless, tanned, long-haired Australians slumped on the couches, we could have been in any beach shack anywhere in Australia. But we were in Oklahoma, a world away. We must have been chatting for five minutes before any of us noticed that Coach had slipped out the door. He may well have sensed that I would be just fine in the company of my compatriots.

***

Our very first team training session was the next day. Due to the icy weather, we were forced to practice indoors at Ponca City, less than an hour drive from Stillwater. As we neared the tennis centre, among fluffy snow, more oil wells, and little else, appeared a casino on the blank plains of Oklahoma.

Daniel, a wealth of knowledge, explained the unusual sight. 'That casino belongs to the Native Americans in the region. A percentage of the revenue goes back into the community, tax-free and these casinos make millions.'

These random facts from the encyclopaedia of Daniel would become the norm in the weeks that followed.

Against the backdrop of the casino's dazzling lights was a dome-shaped annex, depressingly grey in colour. Inside were four tennis courts.

Strangely, I wasn't nervous about my first session. Maybe it was the fact that I was given new bags, shoes, training gear and racquets right before walking on court. I'd hardly ever received anything for free before; back in Australia this would have cost my family well over a thousand dollars. But here, it was different. This was America. This was college tennis where college sporting teams boasted very healthy budgets.

The session itself was unforgettable, but for all the wrong reasons. As I warmed up next to Brad, I felt strange in the new environment.

'Mate, is it normal for the ball to skid through the court like this?' I asked him.

'Better get used to it Batesy – all indoor courts will make the ball travel faster.'

The sound of each ball I struck echoed, and as great as it sounded, that threw me off too.

'Mate, do you get used to this bloody echo every time you hit a ball?'

Brad just laughed in response and ruffled my hair on his way to retrieve some balls at the back of the court.

Everything was new – the balls were travelling faster which meant that the technique of movement and positioning needed to be quite different from playing outdoors. I had to stay lower and use a shorter backswing to counter the shallow, faster bounce. My racquets were brand new with a different brand of strings to adapt to. To a social player these subtleties may have little impact but for me having played for hours every day for a few years now, every little change meant that some kind of adaptation needed to be made to my strokes, my footwork, and movements in order to keep the ball back in play. That was the idea of the game, after all.

With every unforced error I felt the eyes of Coach piercing through the back of my head. Coach's style was one of management by volume and it was undoubtedly the loudest session I'd ever witnessed. It was mostly a positive tone on this occasion, but it was just another thing I knew I would need to adjust to.

'How are you finding it?' Without giving me a chance to answer, Coach fired another question. 'Much harder indoors than in sunny, hot Australia, right?'

'Yeah, not easy, Coach, but I'll figure it out soon.' Under my breath, I added, 'I hope.'

'Of course, you will. You're too good of a player not to be able to adjust. The great players adjust quickly.'

I wasn't sure if he meant that I was a great player or not by that statement. 'Well, I guess I will adjust quickly then,' I half joked.

Coach gave a wink and a smile and moved to another court.

He was kind to me. He knew I was going to take some time to adjust, so he said nothing to me the rest of the session. That made me feel better, at least for a few minutes. By the end of the session though, I was spent emotionally. Physically, I hadn't worked that hard for a long time. I was desperate to prove myself to Coach and my teammates, especially being on a full scholarship which I knew was a privilege rather than the norm. I wanted to justify that scholarship to them all.

***

We backed up the next day with another session in Ponca City. One day closer to our first team match of the season, and the intensity in Coach's voice increased. Yesterday's patience and kindness towards me vanished. A switch was flicked.

In full voice, arms flying around in all directions, saliva accumulating on the corners of his mouth, pacing backwards and forwards, Coach barked, 'Ok guys, we've all been here practising a few days now. No more excuses. Let's get to work! If ya'll want to play in the top six, today's the day to show up and show me what you got. Who's gonna step up? Is it you, Bates?'

A series of tiebreaker plays were on the agenda and it was clear that Coach meant business. I suspect that Coach deliberately chose tiebreakers as they were so short in length. He was keen to turn the pressure up to see which players were able to perform right away. There was no time to ease one's way into these contests. One bad minute of play and the tiebreaker was as good as over.

Although Coach's booming southern voice released a swarm of butterflies in my stomach, in some way this 'now or never' edict had the desired effect on me. I liked situations where there were two possible outcomes – get it right or lose. It allowed me to focus on what I needed to do, and actually *do* it. As early as my first ever competitive game of tennis, aged seven or eight, I was able to pick apart an opponent's weaknesses quicker than most players. Often by the time they had noticed my weaknesses, I was well ahead. Today was no different. Tiebreak play suited me.

I managed to win all my tiebreakers, even against my new roomie, Pavel. He was good; I felt that he was considerably better than me in fact. His seemingly effortless serve arrived on my side of the net with more bounce, speed, and spin than I'd ever seen. His movement for a tall man was exceptional. He appeared to have very few weaknesses; his only one on this occasion was that he knew that he was stronger than everyone else and lost his focus. He didn't have anything to prove – but I certainly did! Hardly surprising then that, after that day I never beat Pavel again, in any form of point play or set play, for the next two years.

After the session, having tried to beat each other, we all jumped in the minibus, taking it as an opportunity to switch gears. Literally shutting the door on the session, we set about enjoying each other's company.

'Let's get outta Dodge,' Coach would say as we bundled into the van to leave for home. This, I would learn, was a colloquial midwestern saying about Dodge City, Kansas, the cliched setting of cowboy and western films from yesteryear.

These bus trips were my first time experiencing vastly different cultures. Spending so much time together in a confined space was a great way to observe the differences between Aussies and Czechs. Martin and Pav, the Czech lads, would roll their eyes as we talked loudly and incessantly about the latest news in world cricket or Australian Rules football. To distract themselves from our banter in such close quarters, Martin and Pav would talk quietly about *their* national obsession – ice hockey. Occasionally, they would drift into speaking their native tongue and we often wondered which one of us they were talking about.

When we weren't talking sport, we would listen to Coach's jokes. I often had a pen and paper handy to jot them down as I was eager never to forget them. In saying that, sorry folks, they are too inappropriate for this book. But they made us laugh and that laughter among teammates brought us together.

This was a refreshing change for me. For the last two or three years I'd missed team sports. Tennis was dog-eat-dog back in Australia. Don't give away your training secrets. Don't become too friendly with your opponents. Tennis tournaments promoted a selfish environment. Parents didn't talk to other parents. If they did, hidden behind the superficial pleasantries, they were trying to find out another player's training secrets. Off court, in between matches, I had some good friends and we would spend time playing table tennis in the club house or playing cards. All too often however, once we stepped on court, often against each other, we were enemies.

That was a strange and confusing concept for me, but we had to accept that it was part of tennis. Ultimately, nobody cared if you had a heartbreaking loss or were injured or feeling sluggish. When matches were finished for the day, all players went their separate ways back to their homes and then back into it again the very next day. This continued for most weekends across the year. I kept at it because my enjoyment came from improving and ultimately, winning. It had become part of my identity.

This lonely existence suited some, but not me. I was a people person and I needed to be around people with whom I could share success and failure. People who legitimately cared. In my short time in Oklahoma, my new teammates had a vested interest in me. And I cared about them. We cared about each other because we were a team. We were all away from our families and our normal support, so we became family by default.

We were also extremely competitive, and so we cared about each other's improvement.

'A team is only as good as its biggest weakness,' I would often hear coaches and athletes say on television. I could now see with my own eyes what those words meant. We all wanted to prove ourselves to each other and not let our team down. Even in those early sessions, we would push each other and share constructive criticism.

'Get stuck into training today, boys. The work we do here wins us matches later this year,' Brad liked to say as we completed our warm-up sprints on-court. 'Oi Batesy, you won't get away with that shot against the good teams. Put that back in the cupboard and lock the door!'

Born into my family the youngest of four boys, I had learnt teamwork and the magic of brotherhood. That had always been important to me. So here I was, all the way over in Oklahoma, witnessing for the first time since my earliest years playing tennis, that being a tennis player didn't need to be a lonely existence. Best of all, I had found some new brothers.

***

In between practice sessions, I spent the first week finding my bearings, attending classes, and most memorably, spending time at the Willham dining hall for full buffet breakfasts, lunches, and dinners. A permanent waft of pizza, burgers, crispy bacon, and hash browns emanated throughout the whole dorm, luring me whenever I emerged from the freezing cold into Willham.

I had honed my eating skills at countless family meals where the concept of first in, first served, was my reality. So, safe to say that for the first few weeks I ate what I saw because I could.

Breakfast started with a Minute Maid juice and a sizable serve of Froot Loops, followed by a tantalising selection of hot buffet delights. Initially, I needed a translator to work out what was being served there. A few weeks earlier, if someone had told me I would be eating 'grits', and 'biscuits' with gravy and crispy bacon that was so well cooked it crumbled with one stab of a fork, I would have wondered if I was being sent to prison. But I loved it all, once I tasted it. Grits tasted like corn or maize toasted and crumbed which went down nicely with biscuits and gravy (a heated scone or damper with hot white gravy), which went down nicely with crispy bacon.

Lunch was generally a selection of Mexican tacos and burritos, an indication of the cultural influences in Oklahoma. There were steaks, burgers, and hot dogs of varying sizes and flavours. Further on down there were woks and chefs on hand to cook up a fresh stir-fry. A sandwich making station completed the selection. Dinner was the best because training had finished and believe it or not there was always plenty of room left for food after a big training session. The pizza and pasta dishes caught my eye most nights, but there was just so much choice it was hard not to try a bit of everything.

The dining hall was always humming, servicing those that wanted to feast themselves on the bottomless buffet, those that simply wanted to catch up with friends, or people like me who were happy to sit alone, read the campus newspaper – The Daily O'Collegian – listen to music, and watch the world of Oklahoma State University go by. Students would come and go from classes all day and I would observe from the same vantage point every day, right near the entrance at a large diner-style booth within arm's reach of the jukebox. There I would relax, trying to finish the sports crossword before it was time to leave for another class or tennis practice.

If they were not eating, the students were listening to the non-stop jukebox which showcased the eclectic musical tastes of 18-year-old Americans of the time. *No Doubt, Metallica, The Presidents of the United States of America* and a country singer called, Toby Keith, were the most popular. Occasionally, I would sift through the jukebox and request any Aussie music I could find; *AC/DC, Men at Work* and *Midnight Oil* mainly. I never did stay long enough to hear them, but I always left amused at the thought of the students listening to 5-6 Aussie songs in a row wondering who the heck had selected them.

After a week or two of sitting by myself taking it all in, happily I might add, more and more students would join me at my table, curious to meet the poor, lonely guy with the frostbitten face. Besides my roommate, Pavel, the rest of my teammates lived in other areas around campus. I actually liked having that separation between my dorm life and my tennis life. I was forced to meet new people and it was healthy for me not to be around my teammates all day, every day. Soon enough, I became the 'Aussie tennis dude' around the dorm and I never sat alone again.

One day I sat down for lunch in between classes and I was joined by three rather friendly girls.

'Hi, I'm Candice! Mind if we join you, buddy?'

'No worries!' I nodded.

With two long seats on each side of the rectangular table, the girls chose to sit next to each other on one side with me on the other. Here I was, in rare territory, as a shy boy who attended an all-boys school and grew up surrounded by three brothers, all male sporting teams and a male heavy neighbourhood. Even my male cousins outnumbered my female cousins five to one! I gave a small gulp and my most winning smile.

The three looked at each other, back at me, and back at each other again before sharing a flirtatious giggle.

Candice, the first to speak, wore a bright orange t-shirt with 'Orange Power' emblazoned across the front in black, a show of passion for her new University. She had a heavily caked face of makeup and freshly curled blonde hair. 'Oh my God, would you listen to that accent? Where are y'all from?'

'Straya. Sorry, Aus-tral-ia.'

Megan, also dressed in predominantly bright orange, was equally well groomed, with a summer tan in the midst of winter. Shawna, quiet at first, had a friendly face and a happy disposition. She seemed completely in shock that here, in the middle of Oklahoma, was an Australian. A real Australian. Judging from countless conversations in my short time in Oklahoma to that point, it was clear that when Oklahomans met an Australian, they imagined that they were speaking with Crocodile Dundee, or Steve Irwin, The Crocodile Hunter.

Buying some time to compose myself around my new-found friends, I dashed to the buffet for a refill of chicken steak and potato and returned to three welcoming smiles.

Almost as though I wasn't in their presence, they began.

'His accent is so freaking cool.'

'We should ask him to say, *koala*.'

'What about, *good-day mate?*'

Candice chimed in. 'I know! You know that assignment for social studies where we have to interview someone from another culture? This guy is perfect!'

'Feeling a little like a novelty now,' I interjected. 'Chris. Chris is my name, by the way.'

'Oops, sorry Chris!'

'So, we were wondering if you would like to be interviewed by us for our group project?'

I was happy to be talking to some new faces and felt the interview would be a good opportunity to extend the chat for a little longer, albeit aware that I was potentially just novelty value to them. 'Of course! No worries. I need to duck out to tennis practice shortly, but I am usually here most days at noon. So, if that works, I'll just be here and you can interview me whenever you like.'

As I was leaving, Shawna asked, 'You play tennis? I love tennis.'

'Sure do! Every day.'

'So, you came all this way from Australia just for tennis?'

'Well, not just for tennis. I came here to help people with their group projects too.'

More giggles. And off I went.

Sure enough, the very next day on the stroke of noon, the three dolled-up interviewers approached my table. This was my opportunity to tell a few creative stories about pet kangaroos, koalas, crocs, and the fact that Crocodile Dundee was my uncle (full disclosure, I may have stretched the truth on that one). The trio each received an 'A' for their interview assessment and I had some new freshman friends.

2

IN THE BEGINNING

My curiosity about America was not an overnight occurrence. Seeds were planted very early on in life. My first introduction to America was *Sesame Street*. Watching it was part of the daily routine as much as breakfast, lunch, and dinner. I loved the characters, the catchy tunes, and mostly I was interested in their accents. As years rolled by, I loved all the American late afternoon classics. I loved *The Brady Bunch*, a show which modelled the idealistic American family. Then there was *Bewitched, Different Strokes* and my favourite, *Gilligan's Island*. Maryanne was probably my first crush. I raced to be home from school every day for these programs.

I was also living in a time when Australia was becoming increasingly Americanised. My music tastes, and possibly my dance moves were shaped by the latest talent out of the USA. I was intrigued by the Olympics and the USA's dominance there. The 1984 Los Angeles Olympics in particular grabbed my attention. It introduced to me the idea that we were the underdog and the USA the powerhouse. It seemed that everything we did, America did it bigger, louder, and even better. We had Sea World and Dream World. But America had Disneyland – that far away fantasy land that to my mind was so amazing it was almost out of reach.

Every now and then, Australia would rise up out of nowhere and beat the Americans at their own game. The America's Cup yacht race triumph in 1983 was so memorable, partly because of the enormity of the odds that were beaten to win the event for the first time in history. But also, because our Prime Minister declared the country should all take a day off work to celebrate! Moments like this made me so proud to be an Australian but more so, it ignited my passion for sport.

Growing up with three older brothers, my idols, I benefitted from witnessing and absorbing all of their sporting experiences, misfortunes, and successes. I learnt that cricket was a brilliant sport, especially played in the backyard. Our backyard was our very own Gabba or MCG (Melbourne Cricket Ground).

The main difference was that there was a circular garden right in the middle of the backyard, along with low fences which made it easy if you weren't careful to be 'six and out'.

Hitting the clothesline pole gave you an extra life, and one-hand-one-bounce was another mode of dismissal to avoid. This was useful when the batsman was adept at keeping the ball along the ground, and therefore, could avoid being caught. So, if the fielder was able to catch the ball in one hand after the ball had bounced once, the batsman was out 'one-hand-one-bounce.'

I just loved it; we had our own set of rules and any neighbourhood visitors or cousins who entered our arena soon had to work out how they were going to avoid getting out. When we were bored with cricket, the pitch, which was a concrete slab, turned into a perfect place to hit tennis balls. Adjoining the concrete slab was a concrete Besser-brick wall, with a yellow line painted across at about standard tennis net height. It was big enough for two of us to play side by side. And so, it became sort of like a squash court without the side walls. We would play alternate shot rallies and then see how many in a row we could hit over the yellow line before missing. These were our own games, with our own rules, but they were as competitive as any Olympic sport!

If all this energy and passion for sport and competition was ignited by famous sporting triumphs on the television, then it was well and truly cemented by my Dad. Born John, but affectionately known as Jack, he was a kid from the bush who grew up playing rugby league and was a heck of a tennis player. He was, and is, short in stature but as tough as nails. Rumour has it that he used to play on ant-bed tennis courts near the cane fields of Bundaberg and Childers in bare feet.

Atop his piano today sits a great photo of him as a seventeen-year-old playing tennis, sweat dripping off his freckly face, dirt-strewn from one end of his body to the other. His looks have not changed much since that photo as he transitioned into fatherhood and grandfatherhood. He still has thinning, sandy-blonde hair. His blue eyes still smile when he is telling a tale. His countless freckles tell a story of a happy, adventurous childhood spent in the cane fields and sporting fields of outback Australia. Dad is still as tough as nails but forgets he isn't seventeen years old anymore.

Dad was not a proponent of stretching, visualising, or any of these modern buzz words. 'No guts, no glory' was his mantra, borrowed from Australia's famous swim coach, Lawrie Lawrence. Dad was a teacher, but he was also a footy coach, tennis coach, and swimming coach. In fact, he was really more of a teacher of sport than a coach.

From as early as I can remember, year-round, we would bundle into Dad's Volkswagen, known more lovingly in our household as the 'bomb', every Saturday morning to go to swimming training. Dad taught groups of beginners right through to advanced groups every Saturday for years. Truthfully, we hated it. Not only was it freezing in winter, but we had to sit through all the other lessons before getting home for lunch. It didn't compare to the other sports that we had made up in the backyard. Swimming turned out not to be the sport for any of us. We Bates's are talkers, and although many would say we could all talk under water, the thought of staring at a black line every day seemed depressingly boring to all of us. Dad did coach a few future Commonwealth Games athletes and some Olympians though.

Each day during the week, after a full day of classroom teaching, Dad would coach tennis groups every afternoon, of which all of us were a part. I watched for a few years before I was allowed to join in. Dad taught tennis down near the local Catholic church on a court that belonged to an old, green, abandoned mansion. Dad would coach there in rain, hail, or shine.

When it rained or hailed, we would pick up the balls and Dad would construct a makeshift tennis net in what would have been the lounge room of this once mighty house. We fought our way through spider webs, creaking doors, and passed the odd scared mouse to play in that house. Dad made tennis 'fun' by first teaching the basics. His philosophy is that the best fun one can have is feeling a sense of accomplishment in honing a skill or technique, and that was reflected through his love of repetition. In all fairness, this gave his pupils, including me, confidence that we were getting better. There were no fancy games, witches' hats, hula hoops, or ball machines. He did have one unique way of getting our feet to work in sync though. The son of two musicians and an accomplished jazz musician himself, Dad would sometimes play music and have a whole group of eager youngsters stepping out their volleys to the latest jazz beats.

Dad worked hard and he was so conscious of giving people their money's worth. Not that he charged much at all. He was passionate about progressing kids' development and seeing them see themselves improving. He loved it and still teaches tennis to this day, using the same mantra and same one-liners that would fill a political incorrectness dictionary.

In those first few months, it was clear that I could play this game well and seemed to pick up the skills very quickly. I was put in groups with kids four or five years older. I heard the comments around the court.

'Gee this kid's a good little player.'

'He can barely see over the net, but he doesn't miss a shot!'

These comments, echoed by my brothers, my heroes, gave me a sense that maybe I really was good.

When meeting new people in the company of my three other brothers, they would ask, 'Which one is the tennis player?'

My brothers would all look and nod in my direction and, although I never liked that sort of attention, it further cemented in my mind that tennis was becoming a huge part of my young identity. I took this attitude on the court and I quickly became addicted to this idea that I was 'the tennis player'. So possibly inevitably, in just a short few months after starting with Dad's group coaching, I became good enough to play some competition tennis.

I remember walking on court with an air of confidence and I could sense very early into the competitive tennis realm when an opponent lacked confidence. I would use this to my advantage, and whilst opponents spent their time trying to curb their frustration, I loved the way it felt to outsmart, out psyche, or outmanoeuvre an opponent.

Back then, Men's Metropolitan Tennis Fixtures was a massive Brisbane-wide team competition and almost all players from beginners through to seasoned semi-professionals and veterans would play. It was huge. Dad set up several of his own teams, and he would allot his pupils into various teams according to their level.

I was slotted right in at the base level, aged eight-years-old. My teammates were all at least ten-years-old and my opponents of a similar age. My first season I won every single match and enjoyed reading the results in the newspaper each week. Statistics were kept by the convenors of the competition and awards given to the best performing players in each level at the season's end.

I wanted to win the best player award as well as win the team competition and managed to win both in that first season. I was so competitive, I wanted to win each coin toss and wanted to be the first player on the court when it was my turn to play. Over the next two seasons I moved up four levels where, as a ten-year-old, I was playing and beating sixteen-year-olds and frustrating the heck out of them in the process.

I could almost see them thinking, 'How can this little upstart with arms the size of chopsticks be beating me?'

I absolutely loved seeing that but was always taught to maintain respect for my opponent.

One of my favourite aspects to this unique competition was that girls and boys played on the same team; it was a great social experience and it was exciting being a part of a team that I could call my own. We had a roster that was sorted at the start of the season and I put the schedule up on my wall in my bedroom and looked forward to every Saturday that I was rostered on to play. In an era before mobile phones, the team captain, Glenn, would call the home phone each week.

'Ok Chris, we play Moonah Park Aces this week and we are going to need you to play against their best player. They are on top of the comp ladder and if we beat them, we take their spot and get a home final on our courts in the semi-finals.'

On the phone, I would often be fist pumping at the thought of playing again next week. 'Ok, I'm ready, wish it was Saturday already!'

'Good to hear. I'm going to put you with Simone

for the doubles too, ok? My dad will swing by and pick you up at noon on Saturday. Be ready.'

Within seconds of hanging up the phone, I would get my clothes out for Saturday there and then, three nights prior to game day.

On game day, Glenn would keep close track of overall games won and lost and we would know heading into the final sets of the day exactly how many games we needed to accumulate to win the day. I loved this kind of pressure which fed my obsession for competing and winning. As teammates we were invested in each other's games because we all wanted to win as a team. This, in hindsight, was very healthy in a sport that all too often was played by individuals against other individuals.

Until the age of twelve, I played for Dad's teams which had simple but cool names like the Aspley Aces, Aspley Volleys, Aspley Champs, and more.

One year I took the responsibility of being team captain, managing the team roster, calling the team to find a 'fill in' if I couldn't play, or checking the results in the newspaper every week to track the team's progress.

I remember feeling safe, happy, and confident on a tennis court in this team environment. Looking back now, I treasure the lessons learnt playing these fixtures, often as I approached my teenage years with and against players twice my age.

The seeds were planted in those early years that would grow into my passion for what sport teaches us. I learnt very quickly that older guys did not like losing to younger upstarts like me; so, I learnt to respect my opposition and to remain humble. I learnt how different people respond to pressure differently. I learnt how to win, how to lose, and how to never give up. Dad's mantra of 'no guts, no glory' was in motion.

***

Lessons on Reflection:

That early formative experience can make or break a child's enjoyment or longevity in any activity and can often be a strong predictor of long-term enjoyment and success.

For me, everything about tennis was a positive experience at that point. It was social, I was competent, and therefore I had validation. Others thought I was good, and back then, they said it. Who's to say that if I had that type of experience in the swimming pool, then swimming may have been a hugely successful and enjoyable part of my life?

The problem I had with swimming was that there was no competition or opportunity to compete at that young age. Tennis on the other hand had meaning and an opportunity for me to measure my level via competition. The ongoing positive attention that I received from my family, friends and opponents helped form my identity and contributed to a healthy self-esteem.

For me the winning certainly helped. But that's not going to be the case for every child that tries a new sport and I don't think that was the main reason for my early enjoyment of tennis. I was very keen, always tugging at the shirts of my brothers or Dad to come and have a game of tennis with me. And they always obliged. They harnessed my keenness and a love affair with the game ensued. If they weren't interested in supporting my enthusiasm, the outcome may have been totally different.

It can be something as simple as that. This is the point that is very important for parents and coaches to understand when working with young kids. Kids thrive on opportunity, competition, encouragement, and support in a time-poor era that continually challenges us as a society. Our kids need our time and support for their interests more than ever, and those early experiences can be turning points for them.

***

During winter, amongst tennis fixtures, tennis lessons, and watching Gilligan's Island, I would don the brown and yellow jersey for the mighty Aspley Hornets Australian Rules Football club. At this time, the Hawthorn Football Club, the other great brown and yellow club, were dominating the sport like never before across the 80's. As I pulled on the gear each week, I imagined I was one of my heroes, Johnny 'The Rat' Platten, or 'Dipper' DiPierdomenico or 'Lethal' Leigh Matthews.

I loved that my footy teammates were a vastly different group from my tennis mates. Footy was a completely different sport. Tennis by nature, was quite combative and emotional. I could take the credit for any winning shot but also beat myself up when I missed those shots. There was nowhere to hide. Without a net to separate opponents in footy, I loved the open and physical nature of the game. I loved tackling a player who didn't see me coming and strangely loved getting hit too!

I loved the fact that the coach would lay out a game plan and then all I had to do was just go and play. In tennis, I had to do all my own problem solving on the run, by myself, with no coach assistance permitted. I loved getting a pat on the back for a good tackle or high – fiving a teammate who scored a goal. I loved linking arms singing the team song. It was different from tennis and the two sports complemented each other well for me.

On footy days, there was something strangely alluring about the smell of hot chips, the sound of a post-game can of soft drink being opened, and that unmistakable smell of liniment. Some weeks Dad would go and watch his old teacher mates play for the Sandgate Hawks down the road in the state AFL competition. We gained access to quarter-time and three-quarter time on-field speeches. I learnt some new colourful words in those huddles too.

The biggest thrill of those Sandgate footy afternoons was listening to the captain and coach, Alex 'Jezza' Jesalenko, one of the game's greatest ever players who had moved north in retirement to help grow the Victorian game in the rugby league heartland of Queensland. I cannot remember how good the team was but being there sharing buckets of hot chips with my brothers watching with Dad as he yelled out funny, yet harmless, things like 'chewy on your boot!' as an opposition player was setting up for a kick at the goal to distract him, have stuck with all of us. For American readers, 'chewy' is slang for chewing gum. The idea was that the goal kicker would lose his focus, worrying about the chewy on his boot instead of the task at hand.

Sometimes I wonder what would have happened if I had stayed with Australian Rules Football and quit tennis. I loved the game, Dad loved watching my games, and it was such a meaningful father and son experience. If I managed to get the coach's weekly award, which was usually a $1 coin, it meant the world to me and we would often stop by Grandma and Grandad's to show off the golden trophy. I managed to win the Best & Fairest award at the Hornets in my second year before tennis would eventually pry me away from footy.

As I progressed from lessons and fixtures to full weekend tennis tournaments, I just couldn't fit in footy anymore. However, tennis had provided me a very similar sense of enjoyment and accomplishment. To be good at one I couldn't see how I could do both, so something had to give. In the end, the year-round nature of tennis meant that I needed to be playing most weekends to keep improving, which was especially important to me.

I never played footy again, one of my very few regrets from an immensely happy childhood.

3

TENNIS IS LIFE

About this time, Pat Cash, coincidentally another Hawthorn fan, kept us up early into one winter morning as he took out Ivan Lendl to win the Wimbledon Crown. His famous celebratory fist pump and jump up into the stands to embrace his coach remains one of my favourite childhood sporting memories. No other player had celebrated a Wimbledon victory with such joy and exuberance before and I wanted to be just like him one day, celebrating the sport's most coveted victory with my family in the grandstands.

No surprise then that tennis became my top priority as I reached the halfway point of my primary schooling years. My first ever tournament was the Brisbane Catholic Tournament, held at the home of Queensland tennis in Milton. I played doubles with my brother, Paul, and mixed doubles with a girl called, Kate. Paul and I won the doubles and I cannot remember how Kate and I fared; partly because I was distracted playing with a girl. Girls at that age were a foreign entity to me. I was surrounded by boys at home, at footy, in our neighbourhood and extended family. I was exceptionally shy and intimidated by girls and Kate was no exception. I played very few mixed doubles events after that day.

In every competition I played from school, to fixtures, to tournaments, I was winning. It certainly helped the enjoyment levels. The better I got, the more I played, and the more affirmation I gained about myself as a tennis player. My family were my biggest supporters. Dad and Mum were always proud, and my three older brothers, John, Geoff, and Paul, probably got more enjoyment in helping and mentoring their little brother than playing themselves truth be known.

In no time, the more I travelled, the more I ran out of weekends to do much else. There was no tennis season. It was year-round. I became hungry to win everything, even a coin toss. To prove to myself how good I actually was, I wanted to boost my state ranking and national ranking and set about making the necessary sacrifices to make it happen, not that I really knew how to train. I figured as long as I sweat a lot then surely that meant that I was working hard.

Because of my pursuit of success, I missed countless birthday parties of friends and family and gave up several short-lived forays into other sports.

My ambition inadvertently took the whole family for a ride too. Many of our family holidays went something like this: beach for three days, tournament for two days, back to the beach with the family, practising reflex volleys with my brothers in between beach cricket, international one-day cricket on television, and devouring fish n' chips. I would then take off to the next tournament in the morning, back to the beach that night for some night-time crabbing, followed by a four-kilometre beach run. I would repeat this schedule right through to the end of our family holiday. This I figured was just part of what I did. I wasn't old enough to know if I was doing this out of love for the sport or the addiction of winning. But I did it, and it paid off one January as I entered my final year of primary school. This would be my second interstate trip; the first being the previous year as part of the Queensland Bruce Cup primary school team in Sydney. This time I was headed for Melbourne, representing myself and my family in two national championship tournaments for twelve-year-olds.

I recall, vividly, walking to the car with Dad as we farewelled my siblings, Mum and my grandparents, all holidaying together in Caloundra on Queensland's Sunshine Coast. I was sad, nervous, and excited all at the same time. Sad to be leaving such special family time together; nervous about letting myself and the family down; excited at the opportunity to test myself in the biggest tournament in the country for my age group. It wouldn't be the last time I saw tears gently rolling down Grandma's face as I left on a tennis adventure.

The two tournaments would be played on en tout cas, Australia's closest version to European clay. There were no en tout cas courts in Queensland – all we had was crushed up ant–bed sprinkled onto a harder under surface. Ant-bed was uneven, dusty, and as slippery as ice at times. I had managed to play quite well on ant-bed as I enjoyed sliding into certain shots and watching my opponents get frustrated with bad bounces and grazed knees. But en tout cas was new to me.

Dad and I stayed with some friends of friends down in Melbourne and travelled everywhere by train, tram, and taxi. The first tournament was the Australian Lead-In Championships, the precursor to the Australian Championships. It was held, as if by some good omen, at Hawthorn Tennis Club; a quintessential Australian tennis club with dated brown brick, a clubhouse with a kitchen operated by retired local volunteers, walls adorned with honour boards, cabinets filled with trophies, and black and white framed photos of players from yesteryear. *Maybe I might run into one of the Hawthorn football players*, I thought.

The first training session was...well, a complete disaster. Like, my first training at Oklahoma State University kind of disaster. The courts were beautifully prepared, my racquets were freshly strung, new fluoro-orange grips choked my racquets. My brand-new *Dunlop Volleys* shoes were donned proudly. But I couldn't hit a ball in the court. Dad and I were at a loss.

Dad called Mum who was still on the family holiday. I overheard parts of it. Scratching his head, pacing, and using his hands way more than necessary, he said, 'He can't even stand up on these courts, let alone hit a bloody ball over the net. We're wasting our time, I think'.

As much as Dad subscribed to the 'no guts, no glory' mantra, he also inherited Grandma's pessimism. Grandma is infamous to this day for her less than positive greetings at her door after a tournament.

'Hello daaarling, did you lose?'

I learned that both Grandma and Dad took this approach when they really wanted the opposite to be true. It was their strange way of preparing for the worst. Even so, Dad's pessimism reared its head at the most unlikely times. Today was one of them. Not that I disagreed with Dad; I was pretty woeful. But thankfully, by the time that we had trudged half-way across Melbourne all the way to our host home, we had come to our senses and vowed that tomorrow will be a better day.

It was.

***

The speaker over the courts crackled to life as we drew together to hear what court we would be playing on. 'Parents, players, and officials. Welcome to Hawthorn Tennis Club for the national under twelves boy's tennis championships. 8:30am matches are as follows: Chris Bates. Shane Hurst. Please report to the tournament desk.'

First up, I had to play my Queensland arch rival, Shane Hurst. We went all this way only to be drawn against a boy I had played about fifteen times in my short tennis life already!

Nerves set in immediately, every time I heard my name called at tennis tournaments. I came to expect that familiar feeling in the pit of my stomach, and I came to actually crave it. More often than not that feeling brought the best out of me because I knew that nerves meant that I wanted to win badly. And when I wanted to win badly, I would do everything in my power to ensure that I would be returning the tennis balls and score card to the tournament desk (the winner's duty).

Dad, a nervous wreck by nature, did his very best to hide his own nerves. He believed in me so much and I knew all that he wanted was for me to realise the potential that so many had told me I possessed. Before a match, he would rub his belly, the first sign of his nerves. He would pat my head, smile, wink, and mumble words of encouragement. Then he would find a seat somewhere near the court on which I would go to battle.

Shane's dad was a good bloke, but a ball of nerves too. Watching them sit next to each other was quite comical. Shane's dad would move his entire body like a contortionist with every strike of the ball from Shane's racquet. Less than a year earlier, whilst watching Shane play, he inadvertently knocked a fellow parent off their shared bench seat with his moves. When Shane and I played doubles together at tennis events, we would extract a good deal of amusement watching the two of them in our peripherals.

Shane was very good, but I knew how to beat him. Yesterday's dud training session became a blessing in disguise. My expectations of myself diminished enough to enter the match relatively relaxed. It wasn't my best tennis, but it was good enough, and it was lot better than either Dad or myself expected. I shook hands and returned the balls and score card to the tournament desk. The score card read 6-4 6-2 in my favour.

After the match, before jumping on a train at Hawthorn station, we found the nearest orange Telecom phone box – yes, I was alive before mobile phones – to ring home to share the good news. After alighting from the train, we stopped at a corner shop and sensing Dad's considerably elevated mood, I convinced him to buy me a set of collectable cricket cards. I'd never seen these up in Queensland and wanted to collect the whole set whilst in Melbourne.

My second-round match, the very next morning at 8:30am, was against a boy called Akram Zaman, a super talented youngster from Sydney. I caught a glimpse of him playing on the court beside me the day before and I thought he was better than me. The beauty however of not knowing anybody, was that they didn't know me either. I figured if I fight for everything and hang in there, not many players are going to figure out my weaknesses at this age. I was fit and fiercely competitive which I realised very early on in life generally worked for me.

But this kid was good; very good. His emotions

did not change, he had every shot in the book and his power defied his small stature. Yet, my plan to fight, scrape, and scrounge for every point worked. Often talented players, like Akram, wanted to win by looking good and hitting a lot of winners. I knew this so my tactic was to chase every ball, dive if necessary and tire my opponent. My goal was for him to miss before I did, just as Dad had taught me to do from the first time I touched a tennis racquet. So, when our clay red hands met at the net, I was a tired but very happy victor. There were now only eight players left in the draw and I was the only Queenslander among them. Not bad for a boy who couldn't hit a ball in the court in his training session only two days ago.

My next match pitted me against a local lefty, Chris Draper, and by now I was very comfortable on the surface. That woeful practice session on day one was a distant memory. I beat Draper comfortably and I was now a semi-finalist in the Australian Championships. On the way back to our host accommodation, a tradition had formed. First, a stop in to put fifty cents in the phone box to call the family, talking to all three brothers, Mum, and sometimes Grandma.

'Wonderful news, daaarling,' Grandma would say.

Then we would jump on the train, by now having

rehearsed every station stop in order. The best bit though came before making the last turn on foot to our house; a stop in at the corner store where I had now made Dad a deal that for every match I won, I landed a new set of collectable cricket cards.

My semi-final was against Tane Rakete, another Victorian. Momentum was with me. As is the case with tennis tournaments, people (coaches, parents, and players) become curious to see who was winning and perhaps why they were winning. The semi-final drew quite the crowd and it only made me feel better about what I was achieving on-court.

Tennis tournaments are fascinating in that way – it didn't take long for people to notice who was winning, who to be aware of, who to keep an eye on, and perhaps who might be the easy beats. Soon a hierarchy was created, based on seeding and reputation, which was all too often accepted by all. All players knew where they fit into this hierarchy well before they even stepped on court to face off. When a highly seeded player was pitted against an unseeded player, at this age at least, more often than not, the seeded player expected to win and the unseeded expected to lose.

Put these two things together and the results are often quite predictable. This played into my hands both at this event but also right throughout my junior tennis years. My prior performances, ranking, and perhaps my cocky nature, won me many matches almost always between the ears. Most players were beaten by me in their own mind or their parent's mind well before a ball was struck. This was not my doing – it was all in their heads. Guys with impressive results and rankings were put on a pedestal by way too many, but I wasn't complaining. This phenomenon still exists today as I wander around junior tennis tournaments.

I won the semi final, the final was set, and we were scheduled to play on court one, that court that saw my worst tennis just days earlier when we first arrived for practice. My opponent was another lefty local hero by the name of Steven Virgona. I had observed all week the groups of Victorian players speaking in awe of Virgona as he eased his way through the draw. A handful of parents, players and other coaches who I'd only met this week were keen to pass on some tips to beat Virgona.

I didn't listen to them, although I appreciated their support. All I needed to hear was my mum and brothers' encouragement via the Telecom phone box as well as Dad's mantra of no guts, no glory. There was no need to talk tactics now when what I was doing was working. I walked on the court expecting to win in my own mind. I knew it was not about tactics at this age. It was about getting more balls over the net than the opponent. For about an hour and a half, I managed to do that and the growing murmurs in the crowd full of Victorians spurred me on to win match point and secure what I had not even imagined five days earlier. I was an Australian champion.

The crowd, disappointed that their local hero lost to a ring-in from Queensland, were still sporting enough to rise to their feet and applaud my victory. As I gathered my towel and the balls off the court, I was distracted by the announcer.

'Ladies and gentleman, on-court one we have the winner of the Australian twelve and under championships. A round of applause for Chris Bates who has defeated Steven Virgona 6-3 7-5.'

Dad caught my eye in the distance, and he had a grin from ear to ear. Other parents were congratulating him profusely. It was an incredible feeling to be in a moment that special. It was a feeling that would become addictive. A feeling of complete relief and sheer joy.

I didn't want to leave the court.

I gathered my black bag, the balls, and score card. I could barely sign my name and fill in the score I was shaking so much. After each match on the clay courts, the expectation was that the players 'bagged' the court to smooth it over for the next match. I savoured this moment which allowed the adrenaline to slow down. I gestured to Dad with a fist pump and I could tell from his body language that he could barely contain his pride. I could see his tears from fifty metres away.

The first person I saw when I exited the court was Akram Zaman. He shook my hand and asked, 'How does it feel to be an Australian champion?'

'Pretty good, I suppose.' What an understatement. It felt bloody amazing.

As I made my way over to Dad, standing beneath a blooming red bottle brush tree, it was hard not to recall him standing in the same position just five days earlier contemplating abandoning the tournament altogether.

'Glad we stayed to play this one, Dad?'

I don't think he heard me.

He just hugged me tight and through unashamed tears said, 'You just became a national champion, mate.'

The presentation was held on the lawn right in front of my new favourite tennis court. I was presented with the winner's trophy by former Davis Cup player Dr John Fraser. That moment thankfully was captured on camera, and has become one of my all-time favourite photos; standing next to Dr Fraser, holding the coveted trophy in my awkwardly eighties electric-blue tracksuit and maroon tennis cap with a white 'Q' (short for Queensland) emblazoned on the front.

We could barely wait to get to the nearest public pay phone to tell the family.

Mum's voice was clearly proud, but she was always very measured in her emotions surrounding my sporting exploits. She played down my disappointments with 'it's only a game love.' And on this occasion, she was equally as measured. 'Well done love! What a great experience, hey? Your brothers will be proud of you, but they are all outside swimming at the moment. I might get them to write you a letter to send down.'

'Fabulous news, daaaarrling,' Grandma was heard calling out in the background.

Then Grandad asked to speak to me. 'Son, nobody can ever take that title away from you.

He was one hundred percent right and I've obviously never forgotten it. Nowadays of course, a twelve-year-old national champion could grab his phone, post a selfie onto social media and video call his family to share the news from the comfort of his on-court chair. How times have changed.

I had one day off before commencing the Australian Championships in Frankston. By now, I was so full of confidence that I almost didn't want the day off. I wanted to keep the momentum.

Four days later, I had raced through the early rounds and found myself squaring off in the semi-finals against Paul Sheehan, a Sydneysider, one of the few players that did not play in the Lead In Championships. I hadn't seen much of Paul throughout the tournament, although he was noticeably a stylish, well-coached player. He was also the number one seed. It was a tight match but one in which I always felt in control. After I had taken out the first set, Paul served at 5-6 in the second set and had raced to a 40-0 lead.

I heard the referee outside speak into the walkie talkie to the tournament desk. 'Court three to tournament desk. Court three looks like heading into the third set.'

Little things like that spurred me to prove people wrong and I won the next five points to advance to another National championship match. I was pumped. I was proving to myself that last week's triumph was no fluke. Sheehan would eventually switch the racquets for golf clubs years later, carving out a successful professional career in Asia.

Next up, Akram Zaman. Again!

I didn't waste too much time 'scouting' my potential opponents during the tournament. But I couldn't help noticing that Akram had been practising night and day right throughout the tournament and he was breezing his way through the draw. Hours before our final the heavens opened on Frankston Tennis Club but Akram was out there, practising serves whilst his mother held an umbrella over the basket of balls to prevent them from getting drenched. His dad, ever present, and always immaculately dressed, picked up the balls over and over again. I tried not to watch.

The match started and was interrupted a few times due to rain and for some reason I simply couldn't get my rhythm. Akram was a very tough opponent. He was unpredictable and extremely talented. He played a lot more aggressively this time round and it worked for him. In three awkward sets, Akram got the better of me.

Akram turned to his proud family, and with a sly grin, approached the net.

'That's one each,' he chirped with a smile and a wink.

I cannot recall my response, although I recall feelings of respect and disappointment all rolled into one. Those two matches against Akram across those two weeks represented the start of a really enjoyable rivalry that spanned the next few years. Akram would later take the US college pathway like me, graduating from the University of Southern California, though we never crossed paths.

I would have to wait until the dead of night some hours later to reflect on what I had just achieved over the last two weeks. When the moment arrived, I lay in bed and smiled. The undesirable time away from family, time away from other sports, and simply the time and effort I had put into this sport had paid off. I was a national champion and the title sat very comfortably with me, because, as my Granddad often reminded me, that title was mine; it was definitive and could never be taken away from me. Naturally, the two weeks taught me plenty, not least of all to take absolutely no notice of my pre-tournament training form. Moreover, these two weeks cemented my identity that had been forming for a few years now. I was no longer Chris Bates. I was now 'Chris Bates, the talented little tennis player.'

Next, there was a team's event to prepare for. I was representing my beloved state of Queensland and I was keen to lead our team to victory against the other states.

The Queensland under twelves team coach and manager arrived for the week and I saw off my proud dad who left for the airport to return to the family holiday. 'Bloody proud of ya, mate. Get stuck into these other teams!'

'Thanks, Dad – catch some fish for me.'

I imagined that he would have had a smile on his face the whole way home which may have lasted the whole week back on holidays.

I was shortly joined by my teammates, Danny Tobin, and Shane Hurst. We joined the girl's team for pizza before our team manager, Tom Farrell, called for lights out in preparation for a big week of team competition. And there I was, finally alone to reflect on what had been quite a dream two weeks. Before I switched the lights out, I opened a letter that had arrived at reception of our team accommodation. It was a letter from my brothers, as Mum has promised.

'*Dear Chrissy. You do realise that right now you are the number one twelve-year-old in this place?* Geoff wrote.

An arrow pointed to a small map of Australia Geoff had drawn to indicate the enormity of my achievements.

'*Now to take out the team's event with Danny and Shane!*' John added.

Paul figured there was enough tennis talk, so changed the direction of the letter. '*The holiday has been great. We have been catching sharks, sand crabs, and plenty of whiting and bream. There's a new show called*

Home & Away that has just started and Grandma is hooked. Anyway, better go – the cricket is about to start.'

It was so awesome to receive the letter and it made me very happy that my older brothers, my heroes, were so proud of me. But it also made me incredibly homesick. I wanted desperately to be back at the beach, being a normal kid with his normal family having a normal summer holiday. I would get used to this; crying myself to sleep being away from home and missing out on special family moments. But I also knew I didn't have a choice if I wanted to be the best tennis player I could be.

The team week was a daze and whilst the Queensland team performed to a respectable third place, the week was more memorable for another reason. Mr Farrell, our team manager, promised us a day at the cricket at the famed Melbourne Cricket Ground, full to the rafters with 90,000 fans.

This was a dream come true. I pictured my brothers back in Caloundra watching on the box. At one stage with the brilliant West Indies team batting, I left my seat to find the nearest food vendor. Pie in hand, I turned to make my way back to my mates to hopefully see Viv Richards, the famous West Indian hero. Ten minutes later I was in Bay Eight, police headquarters, completely lost. A lovely lady had noticed my panicked demeanour and tried to help me find my seat.

I didn't have my ticket with me, and I had become completely disorientated among the enormous crowd which resembled a tin of sardines all packed in together closely. I sat in the police station, beneath the stands, watching the game on the TV when Sir Viv Richards heaved a six which was both gigantic and effortless. The noise of the crowd shook the room and I was annoyed with myself that I was not in my seat to witness this spectacle live.

By the time Mr Farrell responded to the calls by the ground announcer to come and collect me, day had become night and I was able to return to my seat, albeit embarrassed, just in time to watch Australia win a nail-biter. What a day! And what a way to end my three-week trip to Melbourne.

I came home for the start of the school year with a national title, the number one ranking in Australia for my age, and a full collection of cricket cards.

Little did I know that tennis was not going to remain this easy.

4
GETTING SERIOUS

I started high school at Nudgee College in Brisbane where my three brothers had paved the way for me. Nudgee was an all-boys school; a place where restless teenagers were provided a smorgasbord of opportunity to let off steam via sport. Right up my alley.

After the previous year, I wanted to be a kid like my mates. I had observed them playing multiple sports, enjoying the camaraderie among friends that didn't seem to exist so much in tennis. Several family friends warned Mum and Dad of the dangers of early success and therefore possible burnout. So, I dabbled in some cricket, but it was never an exclusive event. We routinely had to ask tennis tournament directors for scheduling flexibility so that I could play Saturday morning cricket.

Sometimes, as can happen in cricket, if the day was dragging on, I would have to ask to abandon the post-team celebrations or coach debrief to race off anywhere from thirty minutes to two hours' drive away to play a tennis match in Nambour or Burpengary or Miami on the Gold Coast. I detested asking for these accommodations, but it was the way it had to be to maintain a ranking and therefore, progress through draws more comfortably.

So, tennis was never far from my mind despite my attempts to add other sports to my repertoire. After breaking the pinkie finger on my left-hand playing cricket forced me out of two consecutive tournaments, I had some ground to make up on the court to keep my ranking.

You see, rankings were a result of ranking point accumulation. I could only get points if I was playing. There were tournaments nearly every weekend. It was a constant stress to keep attaining points and maintaining my high ranking. I also wanted to maintain my place on top of that hierarchy that had been established back in Melbourne the previous year. A declining ranking increased anxiety levels because it wasn't just the ranking that was affected. For me my high ranking was all I had known and frankly it was my identity. Good seedings meant good draws, and this allowed me to travel a little further to play tournaments, knowing that I would at least avoid playing another seeded player in the first round or two. Only by accumulating ranking points could I be guaranteed the higher seed and therefore easier draws.

For my parents this made the expense a little more worthwhile. With a poor ranking, sending me away to play would be risky. My parents, like a lot of other tennis parents I dare say, would have to weigh up the cost of sending me interstate for tournaments. There was an increased risk of going all that way only to run into the top seed on day one.

For me, and other young players, this added pressure to perform because I knew that Mum and Dad had sacrificed something for me to be there, possibly at the expense of one my older brothers. So, in my eyes I had to perform to make the trip worthwhile. In essence, playing tennis was like jumping on a treadmill on January 1st and never really jumping off until December 25th. At times I was able to slow the treadmill down to a jog but most of the time it was a one hundred metre sprint, sometimes on an incline.

That year, whilst my tennis game held firm, I started to encounter players who were becoming men as they hit the teens whilst I was still a skinny boy who relied on determination and consistency. Power was starting to beat my consistency more and more, but by year's end I did enough to maintain the number one ranking in Queensland and top-five ranking in Australia. I was invited to the Australian Institute of Sport (AIS) for a week-long camp with the best fourteen-year-old players in Australia.

From the moment I stepped foot into the dark, dull halls of the place I was unhappy and uncomfortable. There was a staleness about the space and a distinct lack of atmosphere.

Our first morning we were walked to the indoor training facility where we watched Australia's best prospects, a few years older than us, going through their on-court work outs. I watched them closely. I watched them after the training session and over the next few days observed their demeanour around the dining hall, gym, and on-court. My overwhelming observation was that nobody that coached or trained there looked happy. To my mind, this was not a place for smiles – if you wanted to be a player, this was serious business.

One player I had watched on television was being touted as 'the next big thing'. He did not so much as smile when I said hello several times. I would compare him in later years to Patrick Rafter, ironically who was never viewed as good enough to be invited to the AIS. Even when Patrick broke through into the world's top ten, he would always give me time and I would observe him working extremely hard on-court but also sharing a laugh and joke with his coach and hitting partners. At the AIS though, the only time I saw smiles and laughter was viewing a State of Origin rugby league match on the big screen during the week when all players came together from several sports to watch the game in a lecture theatre.

Is this what being really good at tennis looks like? If so, get me out of here, I thought.

I was a compliant, well-behaved boy at this stage, but I did have a cheeky, fun-loving side to me. Throughout my school years I was to find out that this was not always understood or embraced by coaches and teachers. The AIS coach report was no different.

The report was shared with me and my parents when I returned with words to this effect: 'Chris Bates, from Brisbane, Queensland. Talented lefty but lazy, lacking intensity, focus, and maturity'.

Those words stuck with me for many years, sometimes motivating me to prove that they were obviously wrong, but sometimes I believed them. These were the best coaches in Australia, after all.

At different times in the state talent squad I had examined my game back on video, and what I saw on video and what I felt on-court were poles apart. I will concede that sometimes my demeanour and perhaps my footwork may have suggested that I was disinterested, but to my mind I was always focused, determined, and moving like a gazelle! So I can understand how coaches may have perceived a lack of intensity. All the same, the irony of labelling a fourteen-year-old as 'immature' was not lost on me or my parents. And I knew I most certainly was not lazy.

Not that my parents were the types to run to my defence in these circumstances. As strict teachers who were part of a diminishing generation who supported a teacher or coach's stance first and foremost, they softened their stance on this occasion, and I could see that they were not impressed with the report. They knew that I had entered the crucial years where so many kids can lose their way.

I remember that night trying, without luck, to sleep, thinking about how I could have done things differently to impress the coaches down at the AIS camp. I'd blown it. I vowed that if I got another opportunity, I would go down there, keep to myself, and try to do and say all the right things. But the thought of doing that made me anxious. Deep down I knew that environment simply wasn't for me.

I liked smiling. I liked the way I was.

In reality, things were changing physically for me, but also emotionally and cognitively. Words are important. An adult–child relationship should be one of guidance, direction and encouragement.

Tough love? Very important.

Discipline? Very necessary, yes.

But fun? Don't even dare!

I was perhaps unskilled in the ability to know when to crack a joke and when to have my game face on. But for a good coach, in my view, this should be seen as something to work with and work on. And on-court intensity can be shown and taught. I could see this as a fourteen–year-old and I constantly wondered why coaches didn't seem to factor this into their approach. I couldn't see why I couldn't have fun playing tennis and being around tennis people.

But, aside from with my high school teammates, I seemed to be having less fun. There seemed to be an unwritten rule that the better and older you got, the less fun you were permitted to have. I will argue to this day that being relaxed off-court and even on it can lead to better performance. But what would I know back then? In their eyes at least, I was a lazy, immature teenager. They were the coaches that would pick future representative teams. My name would have a big red asterix next to it.

On court in competition, until now, I was not really aware of the mental game. I simply walked on court, expected to win, and generally did. I was in a zone which I found impossible to recreate in later years. As my brain developed it's almost as though it invited more thoughts than were necessary. I became hyper-aware of my thoughts on-court and often found myself caught up in them. I am sure almost all tennis players could identify with this phenomenon.

Tennis and winning was not automatic anymore. I scrambled my way through to the Under 14 Nationals, this time held in Brisbane. I wasn't too confident in my game leading into the event, having only recently switched from my trusty two-handed backhand to a one hander due to chronic niggling wrist issues. Not a great mindset. An article was written in The Courier Mail that nominated me as Queensland's biggest chance to win it all. I read it and didn't believe it.

Despite this, I scraped through to the semi-finals. My opponent, Jong Min Lee, from Melbourne, had burst onto the tennis scene that year, beating everybody in sight. He arrived in Brisbane that morning, saddled up on the warm-up court next to mine with his entourage of physio, masseuse, and coach. He even had a massage table on court. The roles had reversed from Under 12s; this time, I had mentally placed myself slightly down the hierarchy and I was intimidated. I fought hard because that's all I knew. But I was out-muscled, out-psyched, and out-played.

For the first time I started to lament this one sport focus. As usual though, my brothers told me to pull my head in, be positive, and keep working. My godfather, Uncle John, visiting from interstate on holidays, sensed my disconcertedness and provided a sit-down chat, inspired by his stories as a transplant and vascular surgeon.

'In my work, I'm determined to make people better, to beat the bloody disease. In tennis, you've got to have killer instinct, Christopher; you need to be desperate to beat the bloody kid up the other end,' he urged.

He would then show me some of his surgeries on film that helped change the way those life-saving surgeries would be performed world-wide. He shared stories of his decades of work that took him from Thursday Island, to London, to Perth, and eventually Sydney.

It had the desired effect to fire me up, and I

entered the next year with renewed focus. I had never needed this type of talk in the past – I had a natural hunger to win and was fiercely competitive. Maybe I had listened to the misinformed labels of 'lazy' and 'immature' and started to believe them.

***

Lessons On Reflection:

The years aged thirteen to fifteen are crucial make or break years. Physically, bodies are changing constantly, so this can affect movement, game style, and energy levels let alone emotions. In this phase, it's more important than ever for kids to have mentors, role models, and ideally family, in their corner.

It's also pertinent to have interests and an identity outside of just tennis. Above all, it's critical to be patient. The temptation, in a one-on-one sport like tennis, is to copy what the good players are doing in a given age group – find out how much training they are doing, who is their coach, where they train – and copy it. I've seen it so much. By the time families have made these changes of coach, racquet, training regime, there's a new player rising up who is doing something completely different.

In the process, a good initial relationship with a coach has been damaged and confusion sets in for the teenager. I've observed this for thirty years around tennis tournaments.

The lesson here is to enjoy the journey. Let it be your

journey, your way. Players develop at different stages and ages. Be patient as parents. Don't panic when results are not going your child's way. Find people you can trust to help and stick with them. And whatever you do – avoid comparing your son or daughter to others; it's a dangerous exercise simply because you are not comparing apples with apples.

There are so many variables when you are looking at tennis development. Key factors to look for in your child are enjoyment, commitment, good habits, and positivity. Let a knowledgeable, trustworthy coach do the rest.

If parents or coaches get this period of time wrong, it can spell the end of a passion for tennis that is hard to wrest back.

5

THE RUSH

Sometime during my early high school years, a significant shift in tennis happened. An era of tennis started in the USA that, in my view, impacted the tennis psyche in Australia for decades to follow. It impacted how coaches coached, players played, and how families approach the sport of tennis. With the benefit of time and reflection, it impacted me big time. US superstars Sampras, Agassi, Courier, Krickstein, and Chang, all around twenty years of age, were winning everything.

The tennis world in Australia went into a panic. With no real crop of players seemingly emerging in Australia since Pat Cash's Wimbledon victory, all eyes turned to the USA. There was a quest to find out their secret recipe for their youthful surge of success. All of a sudden, the explicit and implicit message, via an urgent compulsory meeting for promising young juniors hosted by the best coaches in Australia, was this: if you are not in the top hundred in the world by the age of twenty, forget it! For girls the news was worse! A new era of European youths brought the average age of a pro tennis player under the age of twenty. This was the dawn of a freakish era, likely never to be repeated. But nobody knew that at the time; at least not in Australia.

My entire family was affected by the messages from that meeting. I had won the U12 National title in Melbourne, had progressed well into my mid-teens but little did I know that this success was only going to add pressure. I had developed anxiety around performance and expectation. Now this!

This stress and anxiety would linger as I progressed through my remaining three years of high school.

In my mind, mostly due to the surge in the US tennis scene, I had a decision to make and I needed to make it fast. In fact, I needed to do everything fast. I needed to finish school and turn professional. This was the clear message that my family was told by the best coaches in Australia. Many advised to quit school altogether to do so. So, in my fifteen-year-old mind, I quickly did the maths – I had five years to 'make it'. I needed to travel. I needed money. I needed to get my ranking up. I needed to change my game to match that of the young Americans. I needed a big forehand and a big serve. So much for wanting to model my game on John McEnroe's! I needed to be in the gym every day to be able to generate more power.

I felt that I was in a rush. The enjoyment of the game was diminishing considerably. Instead of enjoying being a kid, tennis became a very serious, intensely focussed lifestyle that was really a race against a prescribed deadline to 'make it'. My parents were forking out more and more money, and in a shorter time frame than they had planned. I was getting niggling injuries from over-training. I was always worried about accumulating ranking points. I was all too aware of the costs of training, coaching, travel, food, accommodation, restringing, entry fees; the stress this caused the whole family.

And it affected my performance too. I felt the pressure of wanting to repay my family; the harder I tried, the worse I played. And all the while, time was ticking. They say time can be a great healer, but in this instance, it was the enemy.

My sixteenth year fast became my seventeenth, and with that, the blur of high school, as important as it was, really served as an interruption to my tennis deadlines. The son of two teachers, I knew the importance of education for my future. I loved my school, I loved my schoolmates, and I had some amazing experiences with the school tennis team, but school passed me by as academics played second fiddle to tennis. Before I knew it, I had played my last high school tennis match and taken my last exam.

My last match for the school, against perennial contender Brisbane Grammar School, is noteworthy. With both teams unbeaten heading into the final round of competition, Brisbane Grammar supporters turned out in their droves at our home courts. Not only did they fill the stands, but they were also joined by a drumline, banging their snares and bass drums at every permitted opportunity. Word spread amongst the boarding house at Nudgee that we were outnumbered, and soon after we struck the first ball of the day we were engulfed by the blue and white army of Nudgee supporters. There was standing room only, and the court became an amphitheatre in every sense.

My doubles partner, Burnsy, as he was affectionately known throughout the boarding house, had never seen a crowd like it. At one point he admitted that he was scared.

'What if we lose this, Bates? We have to win for this crowd. But I'm as tight as a fish's backside.'

I slapped him on the back. 'We'll be right Burnsy, just watch the ball and hit it.'

To begin with, we did just that and did it very well despite the combination of the howling and unpredictable winds, and a Grammar team desperate to keep their own drums beating. And then the moment arrived.

At a critical point in the first set, Burnsy struck a forehand volley right at our opponent's chest. As the ball ricocheted off the frame of the Grammar player's racquet, seemingly headed onto the neighbouring court, Burnsy seized his moment. Turning to his fellow boarders, those that had given up their morning to support us, he launched into an almighty scream, complete with double fist pumps, reminiscent of Pat Cash's Wimbledon triumph.

'Come on! Let's go Nudgee!!'

Burnsy's moment quickly turned sour as the soaring ball which for all money was heading for the adjacent court, made a wind induced detour. It was heading right for Burnsy. Despite my loudest attempts to capture Burnsy's attention, the ball landed right on top of his head. Game Brisbane Grammar.

Silence. Dead silence. Then uncomfortable giggles followed by raucous laughter. And that was just me! Soon the entire crowd was in a similar fit of laughter. The moment was just what Burnsy needed to loosen up. History shows that we won that match, and did not lose a match all day, winning a premiership that will be remembered as much for the great tennis we were able to play as it will be for Burnsy's ill-fated celebrations.

Beyond the walls of Nudgee, tertiary studies were not part of the plan. Shortly after and without hesitation, I deferred a university course to study Communications. For tennis players post high school, there were two encouraged pathways – 'making it' or quitting the game. Study was not a feasible option. So, for the foreseeable future, I was going to grow my hair and go for the 'making it' option. I needed a training venue, but there weren't many options.

I eventually chose to train at Coops on Brisbane's north side which had one of the few full-time training academies. It was a transitional year and an expensive one. I hated burdening my parents, especially with three other siblings to consider too.

I worked three jobs; waiting tables at the local RSL club, coaching tennis to younger players at my old high school and occasionally scoring a shift as a mini-golf party host for sugar-riddled kids. These jobs kept me busy, amused, and happy that I was contributing to my tennis dream.

When I wasn't training four hours per day, tennis took me all around Australia in pursuit of the one thing that almost all players out of high school were seeking – one world ranking point. To achieve this, a player had to travel to a series of tournaments called Satellites. For those without their first ranking point, they had to play a qualifying tournament for two to three days. If successful, players would then enter the main draw, with the winner of any main draw match generally earning his first ATP world ranking point. Those with one ranking point would normally be ranked around twelve-hundred in the world, tied with hundreds of others.

There were stories everywhere of players securing their first ATP point and plenty of heartbreak for guys who came painfully close but missed out. I was no different.

Despite being supremely fit and no less talented than before, I struggled with the transition into playing against men. I had gone from being invincible, to very competitive through the age groups, to being one of many guys capable and talented but struggling. In hindsight, limiting my sights to a solitary ranking point seems folly now. What was that really going to do for my future? Set a low target and you will reach it every time, they say. The problem for me was, the more I pursued this one point, the more I had built it up to be a bigger 'thing' than it needed to be. That's the last thing a tennis player needs – added stress. As my first year out of school ended, I knew time was running out. I'd wasted a year. The deadline I was given to 'make it' was approaching. Time – the biggest stressor of all.

Now into my second year out of school, I knew I had one last throw of the dice. I was off to America for some semi-professional satellite events in the heartland states of Louisiana, Texas, Missouri, Oklahoma, and Kansas. This was my chance to play against new players. Maybe I could ambush them in the same way I had done all those years earlier as a twelve-year-old in Melbourne. Not only that – this was my chance to play back-to-back high-level tournaments that simply weren't available in Australia.

There would be no coach with me. That was simply not an option financially. I was going to have to do this the hard way. For the next eight weeks, I played the best tennis of my life. I won way more matches than I lost, but all I had to show for it from a tennis perspective was a lowly world ranking for doubles and ultimately more expense to myself and my parents.

But I did gain something very positive from the tour. I visited and played in eight different cities with host families, some of whom I remain in touch with today. I gained a new perspective of tennis too; safe to say I learned more about myself than I did throughout high school in that short period. I learned that I was curious. I loved photography. I enjoyed being alone at times. And I learned that I really did love tennis after all. It was just a different environment to what I was used to in Australia. I loved America. I loved their passion, exuberance, their hospitality, their food, and I loved the fact that each state felt like a new country with different nuances, accents, cuisine, and scenery.

A large percentage of the players I competed against were 'college' players; players presently at college or University in the USA studying full-time whilst representing their University. Talking to some of them opened my eyes to the world of college tennis. These guys were good – and they were not in a rush! Ironically, in the very country that was producing these teenage 'phenoms' we were told of in that infamous meeting years earlier, the attitude was that education came first and that playing college tennis was a viable pathway into professional tennis.

I started to see for myself a new tennis culture; a fresh culture of thinking and approach to development. I am not sure whether it was because of my negative experience in Australia feeling rushed to 'make it' or because the American guys talked about it so passionately. Either way, I appreciated their perspective. It felt right and completely logical to me.

From week to week I travelled to new cities as one tournament ended and another started. It was like a travelling circus. As players were knocked out, hordes of players caught trains, planes, and hire cars to the next midwestern city with fresh hope of a generous draw. The tour was represented largely by American players but there was a fair share of foreign players from Europe, South America, with Australia and New Zealand having a strong representation.

This first overseas tennis experience was my first introduction to Australian camaraderie. Expat Laurie Warder, an America-based coach working for Tennis Australia, was asked to look after a select group of Australian players. These players were invited to be part of the travelling team who would train together, travel together, and support each other across this particular circuit. I was not part of the group and didn't expect to be.

One day, unbeknownst to me, Laurie had watched me fight hard to win through to the main draw in oppressive Louisiana heat and humidity, incidentally against future Wimbledon Men's

Doubles champion Wesley Moodie. Afterwards he was very complimentary and asked me to join in for a stretching session. He followed up the next day asking me to warm up with the other Aussies. It was a great gesture and made me feel like I belonged. Laurie didn't need to do that but his gesture to this day was the most support I had ever felt by a coach from the establishment in Australia. Finally, a coach who gets it!

As we arrived at each new town, a queue a mile long of players would extend into the carpark, waiting to sign in for the next event. Every time I made it to the front of the line, faxes were waiting for me at the tournament desk from US college coaches expressing interest in me. Apparently, they had seen me play at the previous tournament.

Such were their compliments of my game, I probably shrugged most of it off and put it down to their desperation. It was too good to be true, surely. Some of the faxes alluded to scholarships, to paid visits to their colleges, to racquet and clothing sponsorships and more. For years, I shared my parents' frustration in seeing other lower ranked players in Australia boosted by racquet and clothing sponsorships whilst we continued to fund it all ourselves.

If the attraction of college tennis wasn't already

gaining momentum, the lure of scholarship or financial relief did the trick. For years, tennis for me was associated with rushing, financial worry, and complete career uncertainty. The concept of college tennis to me meant keeping options open for longer, living in another country, gaining an education at no cost, and enjoyment. Finally.

My parents noted a shift in me when I returned from that USA trip. I didn't grunt in the mornings as much. I was happy to share the remote with my siblings. I was happier. I knew what I wanted to do and what I needed to do. I was going to college in the USA, and my parents didn't need much convincing it was the right decision.

The recruitment process intrigued me. There was a new language to learn surrounding college tennis. It was all new to me; a world of acronyms. I was told I had to sit a SAT, sign an NLI, register with the NCAA before I could go to OSU, TU, NU or KU. I wasn't sure what a freshman was but apparently, I was about to be one! Supposedly I had to enter via a clearing house too – that sounded daunting. The 3am and 4am phone calls from coaches were also interesting. Some coaches were well into their recruiting spiel before my eyes were even properly opened.

Back then, I was relying on the coaches

themselves and sometimes the players on their teams to tell me all about the college and their program. There was no internet for me to do my own research – yes, I know I am old! I had seen the types of facilities for myself when I was there. They all sounded amazing. They were all full scholarship offers, promising to cover all of my travel as part of the team, my gear, equipment, tuition, fees, books, food, and accommodation. America; bigger and better. It is hard to argue when you look at their college system through the eyes of an athlete.

In the end, Oklahoma State University won my signature. They convinced me to try college for one semester – four months of my life. It wasn't going to make or break my tennis career, they said. That made my decision much easier. I was going to be a Cowboy. A Cowboy freshman. A nineteen-year-old cowboy freshman wearing America's 'brightest orange'. Best still, I was entering a team with a strong Aussie flavour with three other players from Australia on the roster; one from Warrnambool, and two from Adelaide.

My brothers were as happy as anyone. They had seen me fighting hard to make my tennis work. They had fielded my calls from all around the world the night before big matches in search of their pep talks. From the routine I had formed way back at those under twelve championships, my brothers had continued to field a ton of the calls to share exciting wins or devastating losses. My parents, well, they were always going to support me either way, but I couldn't help but feel the relief in their voices too.

My decision wasn't popular with everyone, especially coaches in Australia. The shared belief was that the only pathway to professional tennis was by turning professional NOW and touring the world in pursuit of a world ranking. Clearly, they had zero to limited support for their views other than 'look at what Courier, Agassi, Chang, and co are doing'.

"Players that go to college just end up partying and throwing their careers away," they would say.

They felt that going to college in the US was the beginning of the end of any possible professional career. My internal thoughts in response were, 'so what if it is? Does that make me a bad person? What If I actually want to enjoy this game? Who's to say I can't be an exception to your opinion anyway?'

So, in January 1997, the sense of relief was palpable as I sat in transit in my folks' car on the way to Brisbane International Airport. Not relief that I was leaving home – that was hard! But relief for my whole family that I had found a way that I could continue my tennis development without the expense and such intense pressure, at least for the next few months.

Taxiing across the tarmac I was comfortable. Comfortable with my decision, and excited by the possibilities. I sat next to a girl from Sydney, on her way to Los Angeles to find her big break in Hollywood. I wonder now, decades later, if *she* 'made it' or not. I wonder if *she* felt the same pressure I did to 'make it'. Either way, I hope she ended up doing what she wanted. My conversations with her continued amongst intermittent sleep until before I knew it, we were approaching Los Angeles touch down.

That physical act of flying to the other side of the world as a teenager on my own, fast-tracked my independence and maturity. But it was just the tip of the iceberg as I was about to find out.

***

Lessons On Reflection

Two standout lessons spring to mind when looking in the rear-view mirror to this time in my tennis life.

Firstly, the attitudes back in the mid 1990s about college have changed for the better, but inexplicably this attitude still exists in some parts of Australia today, an example of how tennis in Australia has still not recovered from the 'make it by the age of twenty or bust' era which is long past.

In my role at Study & Play USA, I meet hundreds of young tennis players and their families. It's clear that the structure of junior tennis in Australia provides personal and financial stress for some players and families, still motivated more by ranking points and less by development. I don't blame these families at all – after all this is the system that has been put before them and they are doing what they feel is best for their children. When we discuss with these families the benefits of college tennis, which is focused on academic, athletic, and personal development across four years, for many it seems too good to be true. Often it comes with a great sense of relief for the whole family that such an option is available to them.

The second lesson on reflection was the process by which I came to choose Oklahoma State. I was recruited by phone and my research consisted of many conversations with present and past players. I think whilst we live now in an information rich society, I think one could argue that, with so many colleges available and accessible, there are too many choices these days! I also think that it's possible to over research. It's quite easy to find something wrong with any town anywhere in the world if you research hard enough. This is why often families will say to me 'we don't know where to start.'

So, for readers who don't quite know where to start, here are a few free pointers to get you started:
1. Develop a list of questions that are important for you as a family to find out from the coach of a given University. For example, if you are concerned about safety, you might ask 'what are the living arrangements on campus.'
2. After talking to the coach, ask to meet the players. If you get a sense that the players are a group of varied personalities, this is a sign that the coach can coach all types of players which indicates that this program is one to strongly consider.
3. Research the level of the players compared to your own. If you get a sense that you are the strongest on the team, or that you might be fighting for your position to make the team, neither are desirable options if you are looking for long-term success.

6

AMERICA 1.0

April 1997

"Dearest Gram,

I feel fully settled in now. My roommate, Pavel, from Czech Republic has become a good friend and the Aussies on the team make me feel at home. Tennis is ramping up as we head to the end of the first season. We have had some great wins and some heartbreaking losses, but it's been so good to share the wins and losses as a team..."

***

Just a short few weeks in, I had settled into my new home. I'd met my teammates, trained with them and I'd begun to figure out how to handle Coach's approach. I had met some new friends in the dorm, had adjusted gleefully to the food and had found my bearings across campus. I had also become cleared to compete by the authorities. My relationship with Pav, my Czech roommate, grew from two words that first night to quite a few sentences and laughs over those first few weeks. He had a dry sense of humour and enjoyed learning key English words that I had taught him.

Those words are best left out of this book. This was becoming a theme...

He reciprocated with some handy Czech words I could use in frustration on the tennis court to avoid code violations for audible obscenities. He enjoyed teaching me Czech tongue-twisters that even the most fluent in Czech found difficult.

'Chris, try this. Ready? Strč prst skrz krk,' he would say, spitting all across the room.

I would practise this over and over until I got it, fluently. To this day, I am proud to be able to enunciate one of the hardest tongue-twisters better than most Czechs, or so I am told.

'So, what's that actually mean?'

'Put your finger to your mouth,' he would say, glancing between me and his English dictionary, his nightly routine.

'Ok, but what does it mean?

'Put your finger to your mouth! That's what it means,' he would repeat, this time laughing.

I flushed red. 'Ooh... I get it now.'

I would often use this tongue twister on court – along with other gems – to admonish myself after hitting a bad shot. When yelled in disgust, the Czech language really did sound angry!

When Pavel wasn't nonchalantly destroying all of us on the practice court, he would sit, curled up in his dorm bed, continuing to read his Czech-English translation book that I'd noticed on that first night in Stillwater. At first, I thought this was strange, but on reflection it's hard to fathom trying to manage balancing elite sport and studies with English as your third language in another country! His Czech doubles partner, our other Czech teammate Martin, had a different approach to learning English. He knew every single line of every Seinfeld episode in the show's history. That was his English education.

Leaving the dorms each morning to go to classes was difficult initially, partly because I was full from breakfast but mainly because I knew the second I stepped outside there was little I could do to protect myself from the freezing winds that swept Oklahoma. Willham Dorm was set high on campus where the wind had little resistance. The walk to campus was short, maybe five minutes, but at times it felt like thirty.

Upon my arrival weeks earlier Coach had taken me to *Chris's University Spirit*, an aptly named fan merchandise shop, to pick up some warm gear. I looked somewhat like an Antarctic explorer trudging along to class each day. It was hard to miss me too, wearing black and bright orange, the University varsity colours, complete with Gold Coast frostbite as prominent as ever.

One thing I never did get used to in America was the internal heating which at first was a huge relief, but soon became a sauna. So off came three layers as soon as I entered a building. Then back on again to go to the next building, then off again as I made it to my next class. This was very new to a boy from Brisbane, Australia, a subtropical city where this internal heating and regular wardrobe swap routine was far from necessary.

A requirement to be eligible to compete as a student-athlete in the USA college system was to complete a minimum of twelve weekly campus contact hours which equated to four subjects every semester. These classes were expertly timetabled so that all members of our tennis roster completed their classes before lunch every day, leaving the afternoon free for practise, or as I was about to find out soon, travel.

I won't ever forget my first semester of classes. I had no idea what I wanted to study, so my designated academic advisor arranged for me to be in a range of elective subjects. I must have mentioned on the phone, one early morning back in Australia when Coach had called, that I came from a family of teachers. Evidently this message filtered through to my academic advisor who subsequently placed me into a Physical Education teaching class.

I would spend a morning learning about motor skills, then off to Theatre class to study *Death of a Salesman*. Then, off to the Student Union, the buzzing hub of the University, for a short break from the infamous Oklahoma wind chill before going to my Freshman Composition class. This wasn't just any writing class – it was the International writing class, for those from countries where English is not the native tongue!

In the rush of admissions, I was flagged as an International and automatically slotted into a class where completing a few sentences of English was seen as genius. At first, I sat there quietly, waiting for the professor to pick up on the glitch. I don't know how, but she didn't. Possibly because when asked to speak I spoke particularly slowly so as to not blow my cover.

'Chris, down the back. Perhaps you might like to read the next stanza of the poem?' Professor Stubbins would ask, before turning her back on the class to prepare some notes on the blackboard as she listened.

'Um... err... ok. In this... land... of plenty. The hop... hope... of the world. In the words, the mea... mean... meaning.'

My attempt was good enough for Professor Stubbins to turn back around, lean forward on her desk and adjust her glasses approvingly. 'Very good Chris! Picking up the language there beautifully!'

This was my chance for an easy A, something foreign to me before now. Soon, I was reciting Australian bush poetry and was lauded for my incredible pace with which I had picked up English.

Outside of this class, I picked up very quickly that it was in my best interests to talk. To this day, I'm astounded that Americans find our accent 'neat' and 'so freaking cool'. Different? Yes. Cool? I didn't think so! The accent even scored me free stuff! At Subway, a place I would frequent when on campus, one particular staff member was taken by the way I pronounced tomato (to-mar-to rather than to-may-to) and capsicum instead of green peppers. For every foot long purchase the deal was that the buyer would receive two stamps. Every sixteen stamps amounted to a free footlong. However, I managed to get sixteen stamps on every purchase.

The feeling wasn't necessarily mutual, we had

grown up with American accents on TV and in songs so there wasn't the same novelty. Even Australian musicians often sang with American accents. After about a week I didn't even notice the Oklahoma accent, unless an out-of-stater from Boston or Texas spoke up with noticeably different accents.

I discovered that my role in the USA, certainly in Oklahoma, aside from playing good tennis and getting reasonable grades, was to embellish the existing myths about Australia but also tell the occasional truth. The intrigue surrounding Australia, its people, and its dangerous and strange animals I deduced came from the enormous success of Crocodile Dundee. So, I made sure that my stories included themes from that movie to enhance the intrigue. I enjoyed on our bus rides, telling the lone American player on our team, Jeremy, some of these stories.

'So do y'all really have kangaroos just hopping round everywhere?' he asked, arm casually thrown over the seat back as he turned to look at me.

'Absolutely – they are everywhere. My three brothers and I own one each. Mine is called Skippy. He loves coming to school, carrying my books in his pouch. I feel a bit bad for him being tied up at the bike rack all day, so I usually fight someone for their vegemite sandwich to feed him at lunchtime,' I lied, straight-faced.

Australian history wasn't high on the subject choice list in American high schools. Nor was American history on the list at all in Australian schools. I had no idea that the level of regard America had for Australia was so high. I certainly felt warmly welcomed, even if I was merely a novelty. But I loved it I must admit.

I had become comfortable with my teammates, the coaches, trainers, my new Yonex racquets and the windy conditions in which we played. Our daily bus trips, whilst at first laborious, were so good for our team bonding. In my first few weeks I sat at the back of the bus and laughed as the existing players bantered back and forth with Coach over his choice of music. He was a country music junkie; the man who, ironically, introduced me to a new star of country, Queensland-bred, Keith Urban.

At first, I thought country music was simply a belt – buckle adorned bloke, complete with cowboy hat, singing with a good degree of melancholy about life, love, break ups, Momma and Pappa, and a big ol' pickup truck. Years later, nothing has changed except now I am the junkie. I suspect that Coach now drives happily in retirement in his own pickup truck along Oklahoma's I-35 with no annoying

Aussies in the back seat telling him to switch stations.

Days before my first ever college match, I was initiated into the Cowboy way; the Oklahoma State University way. The team captain, Brad, had decided I needed to come and watch Bedlam basketball. Bedlam was the term given to all sporting fixtures between Oklahoma State and the cross-town rivals at OU, Oklahoma University. This was serious. There were people who would drive five hours to come to these games, and the rivalry on and off the court was real. The blue collar, belt – buckle wearing Cowboys (formerly the Aggies) versus the black – jacketed toffs aka Sooners from Norman down the highway.

We bypassed the public queue to get into the arena, walking around the back entrance reserved for student-athletes. This was cool. A student-athlete was easily identifiable – usually wearing their leather letter jacket; that quintessential American look from the movies so commonly associated with the high school quarterback. The jackets had skin coloured leather sleeves with the remainder in black with orange hoops and a big 'O' on the left side of the chest. These looked awesome and so I asked where I could get one. I was told I needed to complete a full year in order to receive one, so I stored that in my memory bank. I wanted one!

The arena was packed full to the rafters with orange, black, music, and anticipation. We had our own student section right behind the hoops.

'Ladies and gentlemen, welcome to the rowdiest arena in the country!'

The lights dimmed, and the music blared as the cowboys ran out for their warmup. The band played songs that everyone knew except for me, with hand and arm movements in the shape of O, S and U at certain parts. This was surreal.

When the game started, the music never really stopped, and I soon realised by the booing and the cheering that this was some rivalry. This was huge. I didn't really like basketball, but I loved this! This atmosphere was awesome. The music was non-stop, and the athleticism was like I had never seen before. Fans, who appeared mostly to be staff, students, and older Oklahomans, were all dressed in bright orange, riding every bounce, dribble and shot.

The Cowboys beat the Sooners in double overtime that night with the entire student body storming the court to celebrate with their heroes. What was cool was that those same heroes, beaming across the airways on national television, walked the campus the next day with their backpacks just like the rest of us. This was college. This was Oklahoma State. Stillwater had won my heart there and then.

Our own game day arrived, my first ever college tennis match. Icy conditions had continued, so an indoor match was agreed upon between both teams. Ponca City was to be the location and we played a local Junior College team. A Junior College, for reference is a smaller two-year University which is a useful option for many players to commence their four-year college career. Coach selected me to play in the number one singles position for the first match, much to my surprise. In hindsight, Pavel must have been scratching his head wondering why this skinny lefty had impressed the coach more than he had. I knew I could play, and I knew that I had played reasonably well in practice in the lead up. If I were to guess, he was trying to 'hide' our genuine number one from our rivals so that we could ambush some of these teams. I knew deep down I was not number one.

I think Pavel won his match at number two before I finished my warmup! The match was a blur, and I lost.

But I do remember one thing – the guy I lost to had one shot; a massive serve. My strength, partly due to my small stature, was to work out my opponent's weaknesses quickly and better than most. I recognised two or three glaring weaknesses in my opponent's game, but I just couldn't get any rhythm on the fast courts.

It was frustrating to be in a tight match against a guy I knew I was better than. I just couldn't expose his weaknesses because his serve was just so dominant. Some of my better college wins later on would be indoors, but for now I had decided that it simply didn't suit my game. In hindsight, of course this was the wrong mindset. My mindset needed to be one of adapting and problem solving, skills at which I wasn't particularly adept at that moment. Instead I chose the easy way out, making excuses that I would just wait until we played outdoors to show my true ability. I was shattered; the team won comfortably, and that was good, but I was the only player to experience a loss. My first match and a loss.

We were soon on the bus and singing team songs and trying to drown out Coach's country music. That was one thing that was so different to what I was accustomed to. Back home, playing for myself, I would win alone and lose alone. Playing tennis in this team, we would win some, we would lose some. But we would do both as a team. Coach turned the music down halfway home and asked us to vote on our choice of dinner. Dinner was Italian on this occasion; the beginning of a love affair with the *Olive Garden* chain.

This wasn't how I thought it was going to be. Walking onto the bus, I genuinely believed that Coach would be disappointed in me. If his pre-match speeches and nerves were anything to go by, I expected a long speech post-match. On this occasion, Coach said, 'Good job guys', but that was about it.

We never discussed my match publicly or privately. He liked to amp us up before a match and during, but as soon as we shook hands as losers or winners, we jumped on a plane or bus and moved on quickly. The lesson here was that sometimes there is no need to analyse every loss. Sometimes, the less said the better. It's ok to just lose. After all, a tennis match is a two-horse race with one guaranteed loser. This would take me years to adopt myself when reflecting on my on-court performance. For now, I was still in the habit of paralysis by self-analysis as I lay in bed the night of any loss.

I didn't sleep particularly well that night. I felt I'd let myself – and the team – down. I hated losing and I just wanted to replay that match. So, I did, in my head, all night. I did this for many years as a youngster, playing the match in my head before the match and then replaying key moments in my head afterwards. I certainly slept better after a win, but I would always run through a mental post-mortem, almost subconsciously. This was often useful, as it would reveal things that I could work on with my game the following day, but it was often at the expense of valuable sleep which probably countered any positives taken from such a habit.

Our next match was the very next day and Coach persisted with me in the number one slot. This time I played a much better player from New Mexico State University. My level lifted, but the result was the same. Again, the team got up, but I went down. I think at this stage, given that I had arrived with such a healthy scholarship and expectation, my individual performances were at the forefront of my mind. I was so disappointed. I knew I was better than this.

Coach was really good to me on game day – supportive and encouraging. At practice it was different. Coach seemed to me to have two areas that he turned all of his attention to; serving and volleying. It was at practice that I saw the best and worst of Coach. He would probably say the same about me. In fact, when my wife met Coach for the first time many years later, Coach was very honest in his appraisal of me.

'When Chris was playing well, he was as good as anyone. When he was off, he sucked!'

He wanted to change my serve. I had promised my coach at home at the time, Wayne Hampson at Coops, that I would not change any technical aspects of my game. But Coach wanted me to get more power into the move. So, begrudgingly, I listened.

'Have you seen Sampras serve? Or even better, one of your countrymen, Philippoussis? Or even Tim Henman? '

I shrugged, kicking the ground with my toe. 'Yeah, course I have, Coach.'

'They hit the ball upwards, using their torso and legs to generate power, not forwards like you Aussies. That's why half this team have sore elbows and shoulders because you all rely on your freaking arms so much!

'Aussies are taught to serve and volley from a young age on grass courts and you are taught to throw the ball toss forward so that your momentum forwards to the net to volley is not interrupted. Did you know that?'

'Well, not really. I didn't realise it was unique to Australia, no.'

'Well, it's stupid, Chris. Stop relying on the arms. It ain't gonna cut it now that the serve is becoming a dominant part of the game. You've got to throw the ball up so that it would land on your head if you didn't strike it. Go on, do twenty ball tosses, now.'

Grumbling to myself, I did as he said. Ugh, it felt wrong, but I did it surprisingly to his satisfaction.

'Ok, great. Now serve the freaking thing. Tell me how it feels.' Coach stepped back so he could take in my whole swing.

I served a few balls; it did feel strange and different, and Coach was quick to point out.

'That's the first time I've ever seen you bend your knees and explode upwards into the serve with your body rather than rely on those spindly little arms.'

Then he hit me between the eyes with his last coaching tip. 'Learn to do this and you might start winning some matches for a change.'

I didn't realise it at the time, but he was testing the 'prove me wrong' theory on me.

The next day, I woke early, arranged to borrow a basket of balls and I set up targets to serve towards. I finished two baskets of probably two hundred balls before our team gym session and I felt extremely good about this new ball toss. It felt stronger and it did feel like I was using so much more of my body to generate power. I was never going to admit it to Coach, but his tips worked. And his thinly veiled swipe at my lack of wins to date worked too. I was fired up and ready to prove him wrong.

***

Over the next week we had three consecutive matches, all indoors. Coach persisted with me at number one in all three matches. The serve improved drastically, but the results were the same. Ten days after playing my very first college tennis match, I had a record of zero wins and five losses. Five glaring losses. What was I going to do now?

I searched for reasons; maybe the food was too different, I wasn't sleeping enough, or perhaps it was my new racquets. Then again, it could be the new pace of the courts. Maybe Coach's style was the problem. The weather? Probably that had something to do with it, I thought. One thing was for sure, it wasn't my fault!

Really, I was in denial. Simply, I wasn't good enough. But I wouldn't admit this until years later, when I eventually matured. Instead I needed to look elsewhere for excuses. To my mind, the coach is different and therefore inferior to what I was used to.

I needed to blame something or someone, even the food, and it certainly wasn't going to be me. I decided to call home.

'Mum, Dad, this college thing is rubbish. Coach is loud and angry. My bed is different. The food is different, and the people! College isn't for me. Even the bloody dunnies are full to the brim with water and flush automatically. I'm pretty keen for you to look at some cheap flights home, please.'

Mum's advice was rock solid. 'Sounds like you need a good night sleep. Maybe ask Coach if you can play down the order. You need to give this more time.'

I fell asleep and inadvertently slept for thirteen hours in my tennis gear that night.

It was at this point, with another week before our next scheduled match, that I experienced homesickness for the first time. I was actually having a ball in all other facets of college life – but my losses stung me. In hindsight, this was definitely the first time in my life I had experienced five losses on the trot. I was not coping with that and I was too immature and inexperienced to know how to deal with it.

All of the 'anti-college' words that coaches back in Australia used to say to me returned. They were right, I convinced myself. I was never going to improve in the US. I made my decision, I think, in those lonely moments in bed, at night, and in class throughout the day. I decided I would see out the one semester as planned, return home, train the house down, and my name would be up in lights in no time!

Life is funny. From that moment, I feel like I turned a corner on the court. Once I decided I was leaving, my short-term results didn't seem to matter. I was no longer seeking Coach's approval. I started to feel really settled on-court and, with the weight of self expectation off my shoulders I felt faster and sharper on my feet and even my racquet started to feel lighter.

We moved outdoors for some matches as the weather improved. I was in my comfort zone outdoors. I loved working the elements, of which there was plenty in good ol' Oklahoma. My lefty angles and spins were ineffective indoors as the courts were simply too fast. For the non-tennis enthusiasts, the elements assist with spin, and the longer the ball is in the air the more it's capable of spinning. Given that I was able to create more spin than most players, playing indoors took that advantage away from me and in my view created a more level playing field. Conversely, playing outdoors complemented my game style but also forced players to rely on their brains rather than brawn. My brain was my best asset on-court.

That piercing Oklahoma wind, brought to fame through musicals like *Oklahoma* and blockbuster movies like *Twister,* was my ally on-court. Opponents that visited Stillwater hated the wind, and therefore they hated playing me.

Even though I was more 'at home' outdoors, I was moved to number two position where, thankfully I was able to get a few 'W's' next to my name. Coach experimented with the line-up constantly thereafter and I seemed to find my niche eventually at number four. I won most of my matches right through March at number four and now the team as a whole had a line-up that worked. I was starting to learn that it's not what number I played; in college tennis, it was all about team balance and match ups with our opposition teams that mattered.

At the time, this musical chair approach with our singles line-up challenged the notion that college was preparing me for professional tennis. Surely selecting players on merit order was going to help us all improve and give us the best shot of professional careers. On the other hand, tennis was a test of resilience out on the professional tour. Maybe this was a test of my resilience. After all, playing tennis was full of disappointments; some big and some small. Losing was a disappointment that any fledgling professional needed to get used to. There could be a strong argument here that the team pressures of college tennis were in fact the perfect preparation for the selfish and lonely dog-eat-dog nature of the professional tour. I was not convinced either way; all I was focused on was that I was finally winning and playing well.

We were strong really from one to six with Pavel establishing himself by this stage as a bona fide gun player at number one. Martin, Pavel's Czech countryman played at number two. He was a study, Martin. He had the most beautiful looking backhand I had ever seen. His volleys were slick and quite brilliant – world class, actually. His serve, well, it was as good as you would expect for a person who was forced as a youngster to change hands from the fated left hand to his right hand. Looking at his backhand and volleys only, you were looking at a top one-hundred professional. The fallout from his hand change at a young age was his serve and forehand. In singles it was a difficult weakness to hide, but in doubles, all of these shots were his weapons. He was a completely different player. He and Pavel proved a formidable pairing with Pav's sheer power complemented by Martin's precision and brilliance. They were our number one doubles pair, deservedly.

Brad, from Warrnambool, was a throwback to the golden era of serve volley tennis. A big strong bloke, Brad slotted in at number three where he gave traditional baseliners a hard time as he found himself at the front court relentlessly. It was great to watch more highly fancied opponents struggle for answers to this type of play that was fast becoming a dying art. Brad belonged in a team environment and being from football-mad Victoria, he brought a footy team mentality to our team which I really enjoyed.

With Dan and Rob, the Adelaide Aussies on the team, teaming up for doubles, it was a done deal that Brad and I would play doubles together. We often played the other pairs in practice and it was often fiery. Looking back, this was so healthy. Every player was on his toes at all times and we took that intensity into all of our matches.

The format of Division 1 NCAA tennis was that all three pairs played simultaneously to start a tie between two teams. The team that won two out of the three doubles matches was awarded the lone doubles rubber or point for their team. Six individual singles matches would then follow, making up seven rubbers in total to fight out.

This was an enormous advantage for us as we were an incredibly strong doubles team. It may even be safe to say that every single one of us was a stronger doubles player than singles. Almost every match we started out with the doubles win, leaving us with only three singles out of the six needed to win the tie.

Rob and Dan rounded out the team at positions five and six respectively. They were strong juniors back in Adelaide too, so we were one heck of a team. I cannot recall either of them losing too many matches ever, in singles or doubles. Rob was a super talent; a champion AFL player in his youth as well as a player capable of beating anybody on-court. Daniel was very solid – very well coached, and he had no real weaknesses. He was perfectly reliable at six, although any of us, barring Pavel, could have interchangeably played in different positions and done the job. For now, that was the line-up and that was where it stayed until the end of the spring season.

I won't forget one of my first ever doubles matches with Brad. We were playing indoors at a country club in Broken Arrow, an inner suburb of Tulsa. Like all country clubs, it reeked of tennis, quite literally. The alluring smell of freshly opened cans of tennis balls permeated the entire club. The echoes of balls hit in anger reverberated from the courts right into the five-star change rooms. As doubles was a first to eight game set, we could not afford to ease our way into a match. Brad served first. He always served first. I didn't get a look in. Our opponents ripped four scintillating, albeit streaky, returns off Brad's serve, breaking us to love.

'Vamos!' They shouted and chest bumped as their coach leapt from his seat to greet them with high-fives, low-fives, and hugs.

Not unlike my first singles matches, the overwhelming feeling was that we were better than these guys. But after that first game, we never quite recovered in time before losing the set 8-5. This was intense; too intense. I, like many Aussies, and certainly Czechs, were not used to such excitement and brashness. Giving Brad a high-five was awkward for me. Getting in the huddle as was Coach's pre-match tradition was uncomfortable for me. In 1997, this sort of behaviour in Australia would be met with comments like 'look at these show ponies'.

It was a fundamental difference between US and Australian cultures, but certainly not a deal breaker. I had prepared for tennis alone for the previous twelve years. This was different. But I would get used to it eventually and I needed to. It had cost me too many matches early on, especially in doubles. Doubles was all about energy and bluff. It was a clear lesson to me that the better or more talented or skilful team can lose quite easily if lacking the necessary energy to start well. In a shorter format of a game like doubles, this was crucial.

Another notable memory playing with Brad was his backhand smashes. He would regularly push me out of the way when a high ball was in dispute. He would routinely dispatch the ball one bounce over the back fence. Now, anybody who has played tennis knows that to do that with a backhand smash requires significant wrist strength. But Brad did it at least once every match. It was great to watch.

And, speaking of Coach's huddle speeches, I am almost certain it was the same speech he used all of his coaching career. We would gather around, after doing the formal team introductions, with our hands converging in the middle.

Then Coach would start. 'Guys, all I want you to do out there today is play hard but play smart. Hustle your ass off.'

He would then build up the speed, volume, and saliva in equal measures, instructing us exactly what he *didn't* want us to do. 'Bates, don't jerk that racquet back. Rob, you too. You Aussies are all the same. Don't throw that ball toss too far forward! Don't fall asleep at net! Don't swing too much on these fast courts! These other guys play great doubles. We need to be on our game. Ok, hands in the middle. One! Two! Three! Go Pokes!"

On any given match day, off we went, pumped to play but bloody nervous too. This was perhaps the biggest adjustment I had to make. I had to be emotionally ready for matches. The intense guys seemed to get the job done. It was easy to be out enthused into a loss. That didn't sit well with me. From that doubles loss with Brad onwards, I never lost a match by being out enthused. This was one of many great lessons I was starting to learn in semester one of my adventure. I was now winning singles, doubles, AND our team was on fire.

We would get used to *Olive Garden* restaurant chain too. It became tradition that if we had a team victory, we would have a nice celebratory dinner there. Have a loss, and it was fast food. That was Coach's way.

With about five weeks left to go, the season really ramped up. It seemed we were hardly in Stillwater. If we weren't on the bus to training indoors, or travelling interstate on the team bus, we were jumping on planes to California. We were doing well, and we were on top of our conference.

A conference, for reference, is a regional grouping of Universities who compete against each other for bragging rights for that particular conference in all sports. We were part of the Big 12 conference – 12 Universities across the Midwest from Texas, to Nebraska, Oklahoma, and Colorado. We had some incredible battles against the University of Kansas and University of Texas in particular. I remember the Kansas guys being very friendly. But when the first ball was struck, it was fiercely competitive.

With a team of players from various South American countries and brash, loud Americans, there was all sorts of noise and commotion exchanged in a mix of English and Spanish.

'Let's go KU, Vamos!' one player screamed.

Like a flock of excited birds, this seemed to set off a chorus of chirps from all other courts.

'Right here Jayhawks!'

'Next point court three! Let's have it! You know how to beat this guy!'

There were fist pumps, high-fives, and stare downs. And that was just the coaches! All of this was within the rules of course, and part and parcel of team tennis; something that not many of us were accustomed to but ultimately, we were forced to embrace.

I've been wary of friendly people ever since.

Every match up seemed to be close, but there was plenty of mutual respect. I played a guy called, Luis Uribe, a fellow lefty. Playing him must have been what it was like for someone playing me. He was wristy, and crafty, and never hit the same shot twice, even if he wanted to. We had a memorable three set thriller at Greens Country Club in Oklahoma City that ended with both of us completely exhausted. Playing Luis showed me that it was possible to compete fiercely but always play with respect for the opponent.

There were always plenty of smiles and compliments shared throughout my matches with Luis which remains one of my fondest memories of college tennis.

'Too good, Chris,' he would say after I whipped a winner past him.

'Shot, mate,' I would reciprocate when I was outplayed by him.

In between, there were still fist pumps and emotion, but it was always respectful. We never played a one-sided match, and so our greeting at the net after each match was one of mutual respect.

'Heck of a match, well-played,' he would say at the net as we were shaking hands.

'Likewise, mate. Too good today.'

In the Big 12 Conference Championship, we worked our way through the early rounds to face rivals, University of Texas, in the decider. I wish I knew how special this was at the time.

Nick Crowell was my opponent on this occasion. This match was one of a handful of matches in my entire life where I was in the so-called 'zone'. The match is a blur and I do not remember seeing one person outside the court space. I had a rare focus that day. Crowell was a highly touted American junior. He was not a standard cardboard cut-out modern player. He was awkwardly talented. He had an uncanny knack of producing clutch shots that were far from any textbook. I had his measure almost all match.

Matches were finishing all around me and soon I became aware that the entire season, the conference championship, would come down to this match. Such is the echo playing indoors that as little as two people can produce an intense atmosphere. Both teams were in full voice, cheering each winning point.

"Here we go Horns!" the Texas Longhorns would scream.

"Let's go, Batesy – stay tough now!' Coach's booming voice would echo across the courts.

It really was a point for point match. In the third and deciding set, I played my way to a 5-3 lead and an opportunity to serve it out for a conference win. We reached what I had hoped was the penultimate point at 30 – all. I served a solid first serve and Nick put the point into neutral with a good return. My lefty angle invited Nick to the net as he sliced approaching low and short to my forehand, my bread and butter shot. I waited for him to commit to cover the line as I had been successfully going there all match. At the last moment I flicked a dinky forehand across in front of him.

With Nick completely wrong-footed, the boys in orange and black jumped, yelled, and cheered as it appeared we were just one point away.

But Nick, and fate, perhaps in that order, had other ideas. In painfully slow motion it seemed, fully stretched to his left, Nick got enough strings on his racquet to perform the most disgusting drop volley to steal what was rightfully my point.

This point is etched forever in my memory. I will never forget it. The crowd went nuts. So, did I, but a different kind of nuts. The momentum shifted in the blink of an eye. I forgot my game plan and was caught up in what might have been. What have I done? I've just cost us the conference championship!

I cannot remember another point. All I know is that I ran out of time to recover mentally from the missed opportunity. I lost. I was shattered.

And so it was – back onto the bus – a subdued, quiet bus with a depressing hum of country music in the background. Through wet and tired eyes, I slumped there thinking how brutally confronting sport can be. An individual sport like tennis exposes a player to phenomenal highs and gut-wrenching lows. Today was a low that's for sure.

No coach or expert had ever put that into perspective for me until, many years later, after playing and watching so much sport, I concluded that the risk of that awful feeling of losing is worth it to experience the best feeling in the world as an athlete – winning. The key was to be ok with that. Be ok with risking that horrible feeling of a heartbreaking loss in pursuit of that winning feeling which surely has to be regarded universally as one of the greatest natural drugs. In defeat, hold your head high if you know you prepared and competed to the best of your ability. In victory, respect the defeated immediately, but do not apologise for wanting to celebrate too. Those wins are special.

Despite falling at the final hurdle, our conference performances were enough to qualify us for the National NCAA Championships, the enormity of which was lost on me at the time. Not only had we qualified, but we were off to Wichita, Kansas, at Wichita State University to play our first two rounds of a sixty-four-team National Team Championships.

This event felt different. It was like a professional event. Player packs, lanyards, hats, merchandise, and fans everywhere. Coach was acting differently too. Well, really just the same, except his volume and his nerves were amplified. Most of us found his antics to be funny more than anything.

When Coach was nervous, he would pace up and down the courts, and he literally just wouldn't stop talking. 'Batesy, watch how this guy here sticks his volleys. He never misses. But he's a big guy so what do you need to do to beat him?'

Bouncing a ball on my racquet and keeping my legs moving like a sprinter preparing for a race, I shot back quickly, 'Keep him out there for three hours, Coach. Bring him forward, make him play low volleys and lob him over his backhand side, wait for the short ball and attack the net. Make him pass me.'

'You got it, Batesy.'

'Now Rob, take a look at this guy here. He can't play dead. Just work him into the ground.' Coach would go through every opponent with each of us, except for Pavel. He left Pavel because it was so clear that he preferred not to talk at all before matches. It was working, so Coach let him be.

To qualify for Nationals, a team needed to be in the top forty-eight rankings in the USA. This ranking was achieved via weekly vote by a panel of coaches. These votes were based on results against other programs, perhaps a close loss to a highly ranked program or a series of less weighted victories against lower rated opponents. Those programs that automatically won their 'conference', automatically qualified for Nationals if they already were not inside the top forty-eight. The remainder of programs that made up the sixty-four-team tournament were called 'at large' programs. These were teams that deserved their place in the eyes of the panel of voters. We were lucky enough to be an automatic bid due to our ranking inside the top forty-five.

Groupings of four programs (brackets) were drawn out of a hat and sent to sixteen different locations across the USA to play the first two rounds of the competition.

We were drawn to go to Wichita State University and the hosts were our first opponents. We accounted well for Wichita State, who had the unenviable title of the worst mascot name in all of USA college sport. They were the Wichita State Shockers. They were actually far from shocking, but we played well to beat them.

Our next match was drawn to be Auburn University, a team packed full of Aussies, including Lee Pearson, with whom I had travelled across USA striving for ATP ranking points the previous year, and Stephen Huss, who would later famously win the Wimbledon doubles crown with Wesley Moodie.

The occasion of playing to make it into what was known in America as the 'sweet sixteen' – the final sixteen teams left in the tournament, coupled by the knowledge of how good our opponents were, left me very nervous before the match. Once the national anthem had been played, the players introduced, and fans settled into their seats for the start of play, the nerves never really left me; in fact, they were only amplified. I found it ridiculously hard to focus, and I felt like I was carrying an extra twenty kilograms such was my lethargy.

Some might argue that is the price to pay for playing with Brad Chiller. In an all Aussie doubles encounter, Lee and Stephen were too good for us on this occasion, so we went into singles with a rare team doubles point loss. We would all have to step up and we needed to win four out of the six singles matches.

But then *it* happened.

THE HEART OF THE MATTER

On paper I was confident of taking care of business against my opponent. But *it* had other ideas. This was the moment I had come to habitually dread before most matches I played in recent times.

Early on, the legs turned to jelly. I was physically shaking. I was completely drained of energy and my chest was tighter than my racquet strings. Then I walked up to serve. I knew what was coming. *It* always happened when I was serving.

Yep- there it is.

As I tossed the ball up to serve early in the match at two games apiece, the racquet dropped from my hand, I made my way to the umpire and my opponent and simply said, 'I need some injury time immediately – feel my chest.'

My chest was jumping out of my shirt – my heart was racing so fast that it was one solid beat like a song stuck in the cd player. My opponent felt my chest and nearly fell over. I didn't let the umpire feel the beat – I didn't want to scare her too. But I knew what I had to do. This was about the tenth time *it* had happened that year. I needed to press one side of my neck – one of my carotid arteries- to help slow down the heartbeat. This could take anywhere from two minutes to ten minutes. The trouble in tennis is that the rules don't allow for a ten-minute break. So, I would sit there shaking, pressing my artery, and waiting, completely drained of energy.

This moment wasn't abnormal for me – I had been trying to manage my condition for a few years now, dating back to one very hot afternoon in Brisbane. The scene was my old high school at Nudgee College. Me and the only two other guys in the whole school that appreciated the game of Australian Rules Football made our way to the open spaces of one of the twenty sporting fields that we had on our campus. Despite the intense heat, we were running around in our sweaty khaki uniforms pretending we were playing on a packed MCG (Melbourne Cricket Ground) when my legs crumbled from beneath me.

I had been blindsided by a cement truck.

Butterflies were breeding in my stomach. My mate came running over thinking I was messing about, but soon he could see my whole body was beating, especially my heart. It was so fast and so powerful that you could have touched any part of my body to count my heartbeat. I had no energy at all and eventually the heartbeat settled back down to normal. I went to afternoon classes before one of my mates who witnessed the lunchtime episode came to check on me after school.

'Batesy, how's the ticker?'

'Yeah, seems all good now. Nothing like a bit of science and geography to slow the heart right down.'

'Ok good to hear.' He paused, biting his lip. Then he said, 'But I reckon you should probably see a doctor, mate. I can't have you being out of action. You are the only bugger I can kick a ball with at this school.'

I'm thankful for that because in truth I actually wasn't scared enough to tell my parents what had happened. *That would only worry them*, I thought. The schoolmate, incidentally, was Jason Akermanis, who later would become one of Australia's most decorated and colourful Australian sportspersons, and certainly the only one of us to get anywhere near the real MCG!

Jason was right – I needed to do something and

that meant telling my parents. What followed was a series of specialist appointments, all of which provided conflicting theories of the cause of my condition. One told me to stop drinking caffeine. Another told me to stop putting myself in situations where I could experience nerves, high doses of adrenaline, or excitement. My initial reaction was that maybe I couldn't watch the State of Origin or my beloved Brisbane Broncos, let alone play competitive sport!

I undertook countless blood tests and stress tests, all of which came back completely normal. In fact, I was as fit as a fiddle. Eventually, one thing the doctors all agreed on was that they did not believe my condition to be life-threatening. Funny how I wasn't even aware of my mortality back then – that thought hadn't entered my head. This was just an inconvenience and I wanted it fixed if it could be fixed.

Eventually, I struck gold when I met Dr John Hayes, a specialist cardiologist who provided a solution and a plan for me. Part of the plan was to train or exert myself with gadgets all strapped to me to try to monitor my heart rate patterns under duress. Normally this would be done on a treadmill with a nurse testing me with different speeds and inclines.

This test was different; he wanted me all wired up for two weeks going about my daily business at school or in training in the hope that the data would pick up some useful patterns to truly diagnose my condition. It was uncomfortable trying to play tennis with all of this clobber on. The worst part was the data box, which was the size of an old, bulky, heavy Walkman. This was strapped to my hip over my shorts with a clip and the weight of it would literally pull my pants down every time I had a particularly long rally.

I remember one day at school, training with a friend when Pat Rafter, who had often trained at the school, showed up to do some routine serving target practice on the court next to me. He was curious what on earth I was doing with a Walkman strapped to me when I played. When I showed him all the cables strapped to my chest, he got the idea. Pat was full of encouragement and support which I was very thankful for.

All of these tests though were to no avail. I hadn't managed to bring on an episode of what was now known to be tachycardia, meaning irregular or fast heartbeat. Christmas had come and gone, and I had committed to playing the National U16 titles in Burnie, Tasmania. Doctor's orders were to try to play with the equipment attached to me. Like a lot of tennis players, I was a complex character during competition. I would often worry about who was watching from the sidelines or what they might be saying. So I spent the hour before my first match walking around with my shirt off so that all questions about these contraptions strapped to me could be out in the open, so that I could just concentrate on playing my match.

I played my first round against the number one sixteen-year-old in the world at the time, Teo Susnjak, from New Zealand. If playing a guy who was clearly more physically mature than me wasn't intimidating enough then competing with twelve cables attached to me certainly was. I lost badly, ripped off the lot and was close to throwing it all in the bin. It would have been worth it if I had been able to have an 'episode' to provide Dr Hayes back home with some useful data. But all I had to show for my trip to Burnie was a bad loss which were followed by two weeks of plenty more, an annoying set of cables attached to me, being absolutely freezing in the middle of summer and a massive loss of confidence in my game.

Back in Brisbane Dr Hayes, satisfied that the data collection was not working, had decided that my condition was treatable by way of surgery.

My initial lack of fear months earlier was traded

with genuine worry once I sat in my surgery gown in the hospital. What a shocking experience that was. The whole process of being in hospital in the cardiac ward with 70-80-year-olds as a young, fit, and healthy teenager was depressing. The only thing that gave me comfort was the fact that I had an awesome family who kept me distracted enough until I was wheeled into theatre. I gave the thumbs up to my parents as I disappeared out of the room.

I remember a rather attractive nurse telling me some funny jokes as we made our way to theatre. I then remember the anaesthetist offering to switch the music in the room to my favourite radio station. I don't remember proposing to that nurse, but apparently, I did minutes later, shortly after receiving my anaesthetic.

I was awake for the first part of the operation. The nature of the procedure was to insert a catheter via my groin to reach my heart region. I watched the first part on a monitor, like watching a worm meandering through my veins. Dr Hayes' theory was that my Tachycardia response was electrophysical. His tests showed that I was, in fact, born with two valves instead of one, which allowed blood to travel from heart chamber to chamber much faster than normal, particularly with the influence of adrenaline. The first part of the procedure was for him to test the heart by sending electrodes into the right area to try to trigger the tachycardia. It worked. My heart felt just like it did when I was on that oval months earlier. Dr Hayes then told me I would fall asleep whilst he tried to burn the 'extra' valve that was causing me problems.

I was then woken for a second set of tests to see if his burn off had been successful. Whatever buttons he pressed to test my heart did the trick. I have never felt the sensation of an elephant stepping on my chest before or since. But if that is what a heart attack feels like, I will be doing whatever I can to avoid one. It was an incredibly scary sensation. The good news is that the tachycardia was not present, and I was put back to sleep to conclude the procedure.

Later, I recall Dr Hayes advising that he was quite cautious with the burning of my valve to avoid needing a pacemaker. I was thankful for that, because I associated pacemakers with elderly people. He then sent me on my way with another message.

'I think we have managed to remove the valve which is causing the tachycardia, however, there is a chance that the nerves around the area can regrow and in some cases this can lead to further episodes down the track. But for now, you are good to go.'

I was discharged a relieved and happy guy and

ready to finish my final year of high school with a fresh bill of health. The next few years passed without signs of any relapse until I arrived for my first semester at college, which brings us back to *that* match against Auburn in Wichita, Kansas.

After sitting down for what felt like an eternity, all the while checking the stopwatch to ensure I would avoid automatic default, BOOM, the heartbeat jolted back to regularity. This phenomenon proved time and time again to be my biggest asset on a tennis court. Such was my condition that the heartbeat would sync back to sixty beats per minute in *one* beat down from three-hundred beats per minute. By then, I knew it was sixty beats per second without counting. I knew what sixty beats per minute felt like and still do to this day. This wasn't gradual – it was sudden, and it was powerful.

The problem for my opponent in this instance is that this gave me an enormous rush of exhilaration, energy, and euphoria. It was a phenomenal feeling. For my opponents, however, they rarely recovered, worried that they were about to literally kill me. It was enough to usually get me over the line. That was why I had learnt to ask them to hold my chest. I wanted them to know that I had a serious issue so that they didn't think I was faking injury to upset their rhythm. In doing so, what did I do? I unintentionally upset their rhythm and had them worried for my life. Not the best mindset for any opponent to have when trying to win a tennis match.

This result was no different – I won my match, but as a team we were soundly beaten. That was the end of my season – it did not hit me until hours later that the match would be my last for the Cowboys. After all, I had decided to leave. I didn't really know why, nor was I convinced, but my Mum had always told me that when I had made a decision, to stick with it and make it work. So, I was leaving, at least for the summer. I wasn't sure if I was going to come back. Besides, I needed to do something about my heart too. If I was serious about being a player, I needed to get it looked at again. In some way, the heart complaint allowed me to justify my departure to myself.

Back in Stillwater that night after a quiet trip back down highway I-35, the guys and girls team got together to have an end of season debrief which involved a BBQ and game of cricket on the street with a lot of confused onlookers. The boys on the team, as if worried that I may not return after my trip home, reminded me that our team would be unchanged for one more year and that we had the chance to do something special together as a team next season. All five guys besides me had one year of eligibility left, and they all told me they wanted me to come back. It made me feel great, but I wasn't sure.

A week later, having completed all assessments, I packed up, said some goodbyes, and took off to the airport. On the plane trip, the excitement of being home and seeing my mates and family again shielded me from any second thoughts of leaving Oklahoma.

8

HOME AGAIN

"The great romance of travel took a young bloke by the hand –

to the place that he was missing –

to his home –

the lucky land."

Rupert McCall, 1998

***

There's nothing quite like that last descent into Brisbane. I felt safe; I felt I was back where I belonged. It was home and always will be. Dad and Mum were there; Dad with a broad smile and a watery set of eyes, and Mum trying her best to avoid a public display of emotion. Complete opposites, those two. I treasured the feeling of emerging from the air-conditioned terminal into the Brisbane humidity. It felt like home and comforted me every time. I can't recall the conversation in the car; there was plenty to discuss but we had pies and sausage rolls to collect first, a much-awaited homecoming craving.

There I was, back in my bedroom that hadn't changed since I had left, talking to my brother, Paul, with whom I had shared the room for most of my childhood. As I unpacked, I showed him every item I had accumulated in my short American stay. Nike gear from head to toe, collectables and photos to share. There and then, not two hours back from my long-haul flight, I caught myself speaking so glowingly of my adventure. All Paul could offer was 'awesome!' with every new story or photo. I think he was in shock at how much I had experienced in just four months.

A week later, after pleasant visits and catch ups with Grandma, some school mates, and some tennis mates, the reality of the last four fantastic months spent abroad began to consume me. I was missing Oklahoma. Incredibly, though, the 'making it' voices were becoming so much louder in Australia. It was such a powerful voice that it would continue to rear its head for a while yet.

Thankfully, my big brother John's wedding was

fast approaching, along with some important appointments with the other John, Dr John Hayes. These events would help distract me from important decision making, something I was consciously avoiding.

The winter wedding festival came and went; an extremely enjoyable occasion which was a great chance to spend time with my huge extended family of cousins and family friends.

A date was set for some more surgery with Dr Hayes – his conservative first up approach to my heart procedure a few years earlier proved himself right; the nerves had indeed started to regrow, and the identical procedure was required again. This time he was less conservative, and he was confident that I could enjoy an incident-free tennis career from here on in.

My heart was mended, but my mind was all over the place. Everywhere I went, people asked me how my US experience was going. My answers extended to ten to fifteen minutes at times, telling stories with great passion about my short stay. These were met with expressions of well-intended jealousy, almost in awe of the journey I had just begun.

In tennis circles though, I was being judged. The 'making it' clock was ticking. I was being discouraged from returning to the US. There were 'no other' pathways. Just as the humid Brisbane air was in such stark contrast to the Oklahoma winds, so too were the attitudes towards my tennis career.

When I started tennis, I played to enjoy, to compete, to win, and meet friends. On reflection, sometimes I wonder what would have happened if I wasn't doing so well at a young age. Just enjoying the game. Now, here I was, an accomplished player, with no options or so it seemed – make it or quit. These were the two pathways. I had heard this for twelve years, and it didn't take long for these voices to dominate my thoughts, almost as soon as I cleared customs. These internal and external conversations didn't exist in the US. To my mind, they had a different and infinitely better approach to tennis development.

Regardless of my playing future, I was a committed tennis player, so I needed to get back on court. Although Wayne Hampson, my last coach prior to college, was conveniently down the road at Coops, I was encouraged by some tennis friends to make a move interstate to train and learn from a brand-new coach. This move would prevent me from returning to Oklahoma for the start of the August semester. I knew my teammates wanted me back for the January semester, which was the main season, so I figured the move to Wollongong at least bought me some time. Time to keep working hard, and time to avoid making decisions.

My new coach was Ray Kelly, a coach from Queensland who I had looked up to for many years. I had heard he had a great set up in the 'Gong. There, for the next three months, I gained a new level of fitness, confidence, and structure. I had a coach who believed in me and told me so. I became very disciplined. 'Kelly' as he was known, told me I could 'be anything', and I started to believe it. I became supremely fit, very focused, and once again thoughts of making it started to creep back into my reckoning.

After three intense months of focus and training I ventured to Indonesia with a group of Aussie players, including my doubles partner, Paul Hanley, to play satellite events for eight weeks. As was the case right throughout my tennis journey, the sport had a funny way of telling me I wasn't quite cut out for it just when I thought I was ready to make my move.

Indonesia was an incredible culture shock for me, and one which I could have done without. Yet, if this is what I needed to do to be a real player, I needed to be there. I needed the world ranking.

'Don't drink the water,' I was told.

I brushed my teeth and washed my hands with bottled water. I successfully avoided the street vans selling food, as inviting as they appeared. The night before a huge match, a match where I could finally seize my world ranking, I visited a local Jakarta Sizzler restaurant, along with players who had converged from all over the world. Eating the salad seemed the responsible thing to do, except for the fact that of course the salad was not washed with bottled water. I was up all night violently ill and despite intermittent periods of relief, entered my biggest match five kilograms lighter than the day before.

The match was one-sided, in my favour, against a Thai player. I was very weak, but I could see that my opponent was too. I could see him holding his stomach from time to time. It appeared he had suffered the same fate I had the night before. As the sickly hot day ticked passed noon, the match was in my hands when my opponent and I found ourselves in desperate need of a toilet. With none seemingly open or in existence at the venue, at one point we were both off court, hiding in separate bushes trying to overcome the illness that had beset us.

This became the routine on the change of ends for the remainder of the match; a hopelessly laughable situation which ended very badly for me on the wrong end of the score line. In the interests of hygiene, we avoided shaking hands after that match but acknowledged each other's efforts despite our cruel inflictions. I had contributed to the first ATP point attained by Paradorn Srichapan, who would later go on to have a successful career peaking inside the world's top ten players.

The remaining seven weeks were a heck of a lesson in resilience and persistence; the long weeks of practice in preparation for the next event, all the while watching the main draw matches, yearning for that opportunity again, lamenting a tough draw, watching players that I felt I could surely beat if drawn against them instead. This was part of the tennis life. It was hardly the rockstar lifestyle it was cracked up to be.

Back in Brisbane at home, the house was awoken at 3am by the phone. It was Coach.

'How was your heart operation?'

'Great Coach, all clear. I've been playing for the past few months and the doctor is happy.'

'Great news, great news. Well then, as you know the other guys have one more spring season left in their college career.'

'Yes, Coach.'

'They are all playing well and are pumped for a big season. I think we can do some great things with you back here. Will you come back here for one more season?'

I had successfully avoided thoughts of returning to college for the past few months. It was only hearing Coach's voice again that forced me to make a decision. I liked what he said about 'one more season' – effectively four more months. I was so scared to commit to the whole journey to college graduation. I was playing well without luck and felt that surely my luck was going to change. I had a great coach, I was fit and strong, and with a clean bill of health. On the other hand, I knew my parents could do with another four months respite financially.

"The answer's yes, Coach – I will come back for one more season, but then I'm back out again and I'm going to be ready to make it on the tour."

***

Lessons On Reflection:

I still wasn't convinced about college. The importance of the overall education of being at college hadn't dawned on me even at this point. The value was not clear. Thoughts of 'making it' were never too far away. Writing now about those first two semesters makes me cringe somewhat on reflection because now it's so clear to me what the right path for me was all along. However, I'm also smiling because it was all part of my journey.

9

PLAY TWO - BACK TO COLLEGE

February 1998

"*Dear Gram,*

It was easier leaving home this time for some reason. I'm excited to see how much I can improve this semester but I'm even more determined for the team to do better than last year. The rest of my team are in their last season of tennis so it would be nice to finish off on a winning note for them. I'm not sure when I will be home next, but please keep writing – I always look forward to your letters..."

***

The trip back to Oklahoma was easier this time

– I was excited again to provide some relief to my parent's bank balance but I was equally motivated to keep improving. My teammates had four months of their college journey remaining, and there was something special and alluring about wanting to achieve team success. It was a great feeling, in such glorious contrast to the Indonesian experience months earlier.

This time there was nothing new to adapt to, except moving out of the dorm and into the 'Aussie House' on Monroe Street. It was a superbly located accommodation, set just off campus a stone's throw from the beautiful Theta Pond, which was at this point frozen over. We were in what could be described as the Greek quarter – fraternities and sororities in every direction. There was no shortage of activity up and down the street. One block down from us was the 'Strip' – a line of bars, pubs, and the occasional hole-in-the-wall burger joint which gleefully offered deep fried everything for those departing the bars for the night or for poor students like most of us looking for cheap food.

The jewel of the strip was the gross yet aptly named, Wormy Dog Saloon, host to Wednesday night 'penny beer'; $7 entry fee and unlimited beer for just a penny each for the entire evening. Country music was boss here in the saloon, and I enjoyed sitting on the stool... err... saddle (seriously) back from the stage and listening to the local country talent, more often than not, students from the University, like Jason Boland and the Stragglers, Stoney Larue and Cross Canadian Ragweed. It was in here from time to time that I learned the two-step and other country dance moves and developed a genuine love of country music. It was a healthy escape from tennis, study, and occasional homesickness.

From time to time I would treat myself to a greasy Coney Island hamburger, downstairs from the Wormy Dog. These had to be the best in the land, but they can't have been good for me. Down the strip a short walk, when no good bands were playing at the 'Wormy', there was always Willies Bar, famous for hosting the first ever gig of country music royalty, Garth Brooks. Garth was, once upon a time, a track and field scholarship holder at Oklahoma State University before eventually swapping the javelin for a guitar. A good decision, it would seem.

A few left and right turns away was Eskimo Joes, famous for being one of the world's most recognised brands but more famous locally for their colourful and rather large 'keep' cups, cheese fries, and chilli cheese fries, drenched generously in ranch dressing and bacon bits. If Coney Island was a guilty pleasure, then the Joes experience was a real artery-clogger.

Given I was a late enrolment for this semester, I didn't get much choice of subjects to take. I was allocated a speech and drama class on the far side of campus, brutally scheduled at 7:15am. I was not averse to early mornings, but during winter in perhaps the most infamously windiest part of the country, the morning walk across campus was quite brutal with the wind striking any exposed skin like a laser.

My other classes varied from microeconomics, to calculus, to consumer behaviour. My academic advisor, a Business faculty professor, thought that I needed to diversify my classes so that I could have different options when it came time to declare my major course of study. Knowing I was there for simply one more semester, I was not particularly bothered what I studied at that point, so I didn't argue with him at all. Fate would later define this a key moment in my life and future career.

On-court, it was business as usual. The first month or two of the spring season was traditionally cold with the ever-present threat of wind, sleet, and snow. Coach had been lobbying hard to have some indoor courts built on campus, but to this point he had been unsuccessful. Late evening trips to various country clubs as far as Tulsa and Oklahoma City were necessary to get our practice in. I grew to love these trips, spending time with teammates, despite getting back to campus sometimes as late as 11pm. We were all fit, playing well, and our line-up was decided well before our first match. I was number four just like last time.

We took care of some relatively low rated teams early on which was a great way to start the season before the conference matches swung into gear after Spring Break in early March. Coach had arranged a trip to California for the team to compete in some invitational tournaments in Santa Barbara and Irvine. The weather was phenomenal, the tennis tough, and the hotels top class. *How good was this?*

It's an almost unreal concept for most to consider that, given this was amateur sport, we had our flights, our accommodation, our stringing, our Nike gear, food, drink, and equipment, all paid for.

Where did all this funding come from? Well American football and basketball were big money earners with gate takings along with broadcasting rights and viewership making these two sports incredibly lucrative. Their governing body of collegiate sports, the NCAA, earns a lot of money from these sports, with a view to giving back in the way of scholarships.

In a sense, sports like tennis which are not renowned for earning money through broadcasting, really were the benefactors of these big American sports. Their revenue trickled down to sports like mine. Each sport at each university within division one received a specific number of scholarships from the NCAA each year. The coaches of each team had to recruit suitable athletes to their teams and decide how to allocate these valuable scholarships. Some people were lucky enough to receive full scholarships, and others were not. How much scholarship an athlete received came down to merit, timing, seniority on the team, along with the various financial needs of each player's family.

Back in Stillwater, it was a ghost town. Bear in mind that all students in the US university system lived on campus, even local students. Spring break was a chance for students to either visit home for a few extra days, or more likely get away with college friends to a beach in Mexico or a friend's lake house. Lake houses were a big deal in Oklahoma – we were a long way from a beach and so the opportunity to see water and get away from classes for a few days was popular. For international students, we were not encouraged to leave campus, so we were left to amuse ourselves for the remainder of the break until the 25,000 strong student body returned to campus.

This would be the scene for one memorable moment, one evening. With nothing to do but watch ice hockey on the box, the four of us Aussies decided to go for a walk across campus, Sherrin footy in hand. We would kick to each other over hedges and through water fountains, clearly bored. At one point as darkness fell, we could see the movement of a campus police car performing a standard campus lap. For no particular reason, we decided when the police car had sighted us, to run the opposite direction. Given that we literally were the only people on campus that night, we knew we would have looked suspicious. And so, a wild goose chase ensued across campus.

We found ourselves hiding by a Subway franchise just near Eskimo Joes when the blue and red lights started flashing right behind us.

'Geez lads, we're in strife here!'

Rob disagreed, laughing uncontrollably. 'Stuff it, boys, let's run for it!'

We had come this far, so off we raced again in the opposite direction, this time headed for the football field where we could hide by any number of buildings on the way. We seemed to have lost the police when we saw a strange animal dawdling across the street.

'What's that up ahead, lads? That's not what I think it is right?'

As we neared the creature, Daniel confirmed it, holding his nose, and waving a hand. 'Yep! A stinky bloody skunk.'

It's no secret that skunks are known for their pungent smell that they can emit when sensing danger. The smell is bad enough, but when it has made contact with your clothing, it is almost unbearable. Just ask me!

So intrigued were we by the skunk, we had forgotten that we were standing in the middle of the street in plain view of the police car coming straight for us.

'Here we go again, lads!' At this stage we were all in fits of laughter at the calamitous situation we had placed ourselves in. 'Time to run!'

We were guilty of nothing of course, but we ran anyway, this time making it all the way back to our apartment over hedges, bushes, and an occasional confused onlooker, locking the door firmly behind us, waiting for the police to follow.

Still giggling like little kids, partly out of fear, we peered through the blinds in waiting. Just when we thought the coast was clear, there was a knock at the door. Brad drew the short straw as he sheepishly went to answer the knocking that was by now becoming increasingly louder and more impatient. The rest of us listened upstairs to hear how Brad was going to explain this one. Worry was quickly swapped with laughter and relief as it was only Johnno, the British cross-country runner, equally as bored in his apartment, looking for something to do.

***

Spring Break skunk encounters aside, the season proper was now upon us and the spring weather cooperated enough for us not to have to travel to indoor training again for the remainder of the season. Instead we trained in the wind, a brutal feature of Oklahoma. Brutal for some, but for me it allowed my game to flourish and really frustrate my opponents.

As a left-hander with different spins, the wind only exacerbated the problem for unsuspecting opponents. I was able to assess my opponents quite quickly in the warmup, before the doubles match had started. I could see guys complaining about the wind, or getting their feet stuck in position only for the ball to move a foot further away at the last moment impacting their technique. I would look for players on the opposing team that I thought were quite robotic or mechanical with their technique, and would say to myself, *I hope I'm playing him.*

Mechanical or robotic players couldn't adjust

easily to the less than perfect conditions. If I was lucky enough to play that sort of player, my entire goal was to bring the wind to his attention as early as possible. I did this by letting the wind do the work for me. The softer I hit the ball, the more the wind wreaked havoc. The wind, my strange spin, and left-handed angles created the perfect storm. I was proud of the growing tally of broken racquets that this tactic had contributed to across the net over the course of the next few weeks.

As a team we were firing, and it was only a handful of heartbreaking close losses in our conference that prevented another shot at the conference title. In the conference tournament in Kansas City, we outgunned Kansas, and Colorado before falling to Texas once again in another tight contest. It was a terrific springboard into our automatic selection into the NCAA Division 1 Championships.

This time our host city was Tulsa, only a 90-minute drive away. We were hoping for somewhere different, but at least we were close to home and we knew the conditions well, and we knew the Tulsa courts well too.

We routinely won our first round against Tulsa in what were awfully challenging, humid conditions.

Round two was to follow the next day and we needed every mouthful of carbohydrates and electrolytes as another hot and humid day was forecast.

The round of thirty-two match against Cal Berkeley was our chance to advance to the sweet-sixteen. Our doubles combinations had continued to fire the whole season, so we went into the doubles point supremely confident.

Earlier that season, Pavel Kudrnac and Martin Dvoracek, our Czech mates, won the Division 1 National Indoor Championship, defeating the famous Bryan brothers very comfortably in the final. The story goes that Martin and Pav started the match in their full tracksuit in the freezing conditions. After a dominant start, they never disrobed on their way to a resounding victory over the pairing who would become the greatest the sport has ever seen.

My old roomie, Pavel, would also go on to win the singles championship, giving him the phenomenal title of # 1 singles and doubles player in the US collegiate system. Their confidence became contagious and thus our entire team were firing on the doubles court.

Today was no different as we racked up wins on all three doubles courts, taking us to singles where we needed to win three of the six matches to clinch our sweet-sixteen berth. By now, approaching noon, the heat and humidity was suffocating. I enjoyed these conditions normally, although today my breathing was restricted more than normal. It was the same for everybody though. My opponent, Adrian Barnes, from England, was highly fancied and his results throughout the year were strong enough for Coach to highlight him as one of the best players on their team. *Great!* I thought.

I knew I was in for a tough tussle and so I started the match very aggressively to try to take the match away from Barnes. The first set was a blur; again, one of only a handful of matches I can reflect upon having been in the 'zone'. At least that was the case for the first set. It was at this point that I became aware of the overall match situation. This was the awesome beauty of college tennis. We were all playing at once and it was impossible not to take notice of how my teammates were faring.

I needn't have looked too hard, as it was easy to tell from Coach's incessant pacing back and forth across the six courts that we were in trouble. 'Hustle your butts off, Pokes!' in reference to cowpokes, another name for cowboy, our University mascot.

By midway through the second set, it was clear we were in trouble. Pavel looked to be in charge in his match, whilst Brad and Martin appeared to be in big trouble. A pro Cal Berkeley crowd was nestled behind Rob and Daniel's matches and by the cheering it was hard to tell if either of them was winning any points. This was the nature of college tennis. The crowds gathered to where they thought the 'swing' match was occurring. They must have thought that I had control of my match, because there was not a soul in sight watching mine. I didn't mind this normally, but today I was to feel the weight of expectation a little more than normal. I felt we were better than these guys and if I could hurry up and win my match, surely one of Dan or Rob would be able to hang in there to get us the four matches needed.

As I approached the baseline to serve at three games all in the second set, a slight twinge in my calf caught my attention. Slight cramps were normal for tennis players, especially in this type of heat. The very next point as I scampered from side to side, I felt a more serious cramp in my hamstring. *This was ok*, I thought, *I will pump myself full of bananas and Gatorade at the next change of ends*. I just needed to hold serve.

Almost sensing my predicament, Barnes played some relentlessly patient tennis for the next few minutes, forcing me to make twenty to thirty shots per rally. After each point I felt a slight twinge in different muscles.

I lost the game and then, with the score at 4 -3 in Barnes' favour, I made the biggest mistake of all – I sat down at the change of ends. I had to breath and relax and allow these muscles to sleep for a while. I managed to do this but as I rose from my seat my quadriceps on both legs completely seized. As is the case with cramp, to counter one group of seized muscles the others overcorrect and in doing so, seize up! Soon the whole bottom half of my body was in some form of muscular seizure. A quick pan of the surrounding courts confirmed my biggest fear – we were three rubbers apiece and a place in the sweet-sixteen – the last sixteen teams in the entire country – came down to my match. Playing on was non-negotiable.

The second set was now gone, and it was 1-0 to Barnes in the third set. Maybe if I could shorten points and go for my shots, I could squeeze a few games in and maybe the litres of water and electrolytes, salt tablets, and bananas would kick in.

None of it worked. The very next service game as I tossed up the ball to serve, my body went into complete shutdown. I tried, several times to get up and play on but it was not possible. My triceps, biceps, back, and fingers had all seized to a point of being completely paralysed. I was in considerable agony. At one point my tongue was resting on my bottom lip, seized, and cramping.

The season was over. The college careers of my teammates were over. Their last chance of advancing to the next round was collapsed in front of them on the court, helpless, and shattered. The boys came over to help steady me to be able to get to my feet. Barnes, at this stage, knowing the match was in his hands, refrained from celebrating with his teammates to come around to shake my hand and check my welfare. I remember he said sorry that he won that way. I will always appreciate that. The local newspaper would later run with the headline which summed up our demise that day:

Heat, Cramps Too Much For Brave Cowboys.

Immediately after the match, Coach was obviously very disappointed because we all knew we had let a big opportunity slip; our last opportunity as a team. Coach was nowhere to be seen when the match finished. He was starting up the team bus, and it was headed for a local Subway to get in, get out, and back to Stillwater as soon as possible. The only problem for me was that I could not make it up the stairs from the court at this point.

Eventually, twenty minutes later, I managed to make it to my friend's car who was able to drop me to Subway to join my teammates. I was virtually carried into the restaurant, shirt off, face beetroot-red, in peak lunch hour. As I turned to sit, my body deteriorated to complete body cramp once again. My teammates lifted me and lay me out across two tables, each of them massaging different sets of muscles, some with ice packs, others pouring a gag-worthy concoction of salt and Gatorade down my throat.

'Batesy, lie here and stay still!'

'Martin, ask the staff for some ice and grab some more Gatorade while you are at it. Quick!' Brad barked.

'Pav and Daniel, work on his legs. Me and Rob will massage his neck.'

We had commandeered a whole section of the restaurant, but our section more resembled an operating theatre. All the while, Coach was sitting as far away as possible, back turned, catching up on yesterday's news in the *Tulsa World*. This was Coach's way.

The team of masseurs managed to stabilise me to the point of getting to my feet and ready to leave. But I couldn't walk. Brad and Dan lifted me up and chaired me to the exit. As we left a young family with three young kids seemed very confused as to why a semi naked man was being carried out of their local Subway in peak hour lunch.

Sensing the moment, Coach chimed in, 'Don't eat the meatball!'

The young family veered away from us, as if not to catch the bug I had just contracted whilst the rest of us cracked up laughing, setting off more stomach muscle cramps and a very uncomfortable trip up the highway.

A day later having been taken to hospital on a drip, almost one year since we bowed out of Nationals in Wichita, here I was again. Déjà vu.

I was leaving, but I didn't want to. I was a Cowboy. I'd adopted this town and this university. The problem was that every win seemed to confirm in my teenage mind that I was good enough to leave. I couldn't afford to waste more time at college. *I'm not getting any ATP points by being here*, I thought. *My awesome teammates are going, so it's good timing*, I justified. If I was going to make it, this was absolutely my moment. Here I was, thinking that my window to make a career out of tennis was small.

In a rush. Always in a rush.

Lounging on the black couches in the 'Aussie house' mindlessly channel surfing, all of my teammates, again, tried to have one last talk to me to convince me how stupid I was for leaving. I was having none of it.

'Mate, you really need to stay,' Daniel, ever the

team spokesperson, advised with a concerned frown.

'What are you going to do otherwise?' Martin added, looking at me like I was nuts.

I smiled awkwardly, then shook my head. 'Appreciate the advice, thanks fellas. I've made my mind up though. You guys aren't going to be here anyway.'

'But Batesy, two more years and you will graduate and get a degree behind you. Those two years are not going to make or break your tennis career.'

I bull-headedly pushed my mates away by changing the channel to a timely episode of Jerry Springer. 'Oh look, these guys are about to fight – have a go at this, boys!'

They exchanged a look which I pretended not to notice, but they didn't press the conversation anymore.

In hindsight, I was listening to those old voices that were telling me my best chance of 'making it' was not via US college. Not that I didn't respect my teammates. In fact, they all reminded me of my three older brothers in many ways; they genuinely cared for me and my future. I simply didn't want to hear it.

For now, with tennis finished, we all still had one more week of school. Then I would be off to play two months of US-based satellite tournaments before heading back to Australia. It was finals week – final exams. Little did I know that this week was to shape me for years to come.

There is absolutely no conscious reason or explanation for my actions that week. My mind being made up that I was done with college in the US forever, I decided not to study for my final exams. I would do the bare minimum and get back on the tour. History, and my transcripts, show that I failed two classes, one from showing a complete lack of care for succeeding in that subject, and the other for inexplicably failing to show up for the final exam.

***

Lessons On Reflection:
It took many years to be able to admit what I had done that week, but in reality, this was all part of education for me. In time, I came to the realisation that for all humans, our collective experiences, and decisions, good and bad, shape who we are. Good decisions don't automatically lead to success, and similarly, bad decisions like this one, do not have to define us. Mistakes can sometimes be fixed if we are honest with ourselves.

***

For now, I was going to have to live with my decision and set about proving that my decision to leave college after just two semesters was the right one. I had to get out there on-court and make it happen. After final exams, I jumped on the practice court with some of my teammates in hundred-degree Fahrenheit heat. As if to punish myself, I started at 10am and did not come off court except to fill my water bottles until 6pm that night.

I had just trained for eight hours. Not but one hour later, I was in hospital with heat exhaustion. The doctors were concerned with just how much fluid I had lost. Hallucinating and in the process of replenishing fluids via saline drip, I proposed to another nurse, I was later told. Thankfully she said no. This was becoming a disturbing trend...

Ignoring doctor's orders, and without telling Coach or any of my family, I jumped back on court the very next day before heading down the highway for eight weeks of tennis, much the same as my first ever trip to the US two years earlier. This foray back into the semi pro-environment was defining. There were plenty of positives over this period. I managed wins over junior grand slam winners in doubles, picking up several ATP ranking points along the way. My doubles exploits were helping pay for my tournaments, but my singles remained a constant mental battle that I was losing more often than not.

I managed to put myself in competitive positions every match, winning some but losing key moments. My mental battle was personified in St Louis

Missouri one day, when, having qualified over the previous three days for the main draw, I was pitted against Ryan Wolters, an American. I knew nothing about Wolters except that he was the only thing standing in the way of that allusive ATP singles point.

The first 40 minutes of the match could only be described as sporting utopia. I couldn't miss, even if I had wanted to. I raced to a 6-1 first set lead and Wolters was taking his frustrations out on his racquets, smashing them into the hardcourt on several occasions. His negative body language, something upon which I preyed in most of my matches, started to resemble all of the signs of helplessness. The next step after that is almost always tanking. I knew that if I could start well in the second set, I was almost home and hosed.

The first three games flew by in my favour as a crowd started to gather. Here I was, on the brink of my first ATP point, in complete control of the match. I had flashbacks to my under twelves experience where these gathering crowds only made me better and tougher mentally. But this was different. I was now a thinker. I had doubts. Cruise control didn't exist anymore. I wasn't on autopilot focussing on simply winning each point. The prize at the end was too big not to think about. It didn't help when one of my compatriots, lurking behind the courts, stopped by the fence to ask the score.

'Up a set and winning in second set, mate,' I said modestly so as not to get ahead of myself.

'Serious? Batesy, do you realise who this guy is? He is one of America's best juniors; Stanford's gun recruit!'

Gee, thanks for letting me know. It's almost as if at that point that Wolters sensed my nerves at finishing him off. Like a tiger and its prey. He had nothing to lose at this point. Nothing for him had been working, and so now he could free his arms, swing carelessly and hope for the best. I planned to keep balls in the court, play smart, and wait for him to do what he had been doing all match – miss before I did. But he didn't. A switch flicked in Wolters.

At 5-1 in the second set, serving for the match, four clean winners passed my racquet from Wolters as he broke my serve to love. At the change of ends my senses were heightened and I became aware of my surroundings outside the court. By now I suspect the entire tournament, including officials, coaches, and players were here to witness the upset of the tournament and, arguably, the entire eight-week tour.

This next game was a big chance to break his serve to win the match because I had been returning serve very well. This game was no different, but Wolters had the answers. In this game, he made his first fist pump of the match. His supporters were behind him. They were aware of the situation. His body language changed to 'maybe I can get back into this match' in the blink of an eye. As his mood improved, mine deteriorated under pure stress and nerves. I was so close I could taste it. But I was choking. Big time.

I felt that every set of eyes were on me, watching me blow it. In reality, if I was to be transported into the grandstands as a spectator and then told that I was to jump on court up a set and 5-3, I would take it every time. But in the midst of a choke, that sort of clarity is difficult to come by. Momentum had shifted and I was in trouble. Serving at 5-3 I got to within two points at 30-all, but failed to convert. We were now back on serve and this was anyone's match.

History tells me that I lost that set and went onto lose the match. I don't know what the third set score was. I will never forget the look of sorrow in Wolter's eyes as we shook hands, as if to say, *you poor guy, that's going to take some time to get over.*

He was right.

That night, and at times over the next few weeks, I cried as I replayed the match over and over in my head. It was a brutal loss.

The ensuing weeks were very positive on the doubles court, gaining some great wins over high class opposition, even getting some revenge on Wolters and his partner Paul Goldstein, a formidable pairing. Off-court, I thoroughly enjoyed spending time with other Aussies on tour; some who were currently on break from college, and plenty more trying to find their way as full-time professionals. When we weren't practising and competing, we enjoyed each other's company, and a competitive game of cards was never too far away.

Towards the end of the summer, the tour took us back to Tulsa, in Oklahoma in oppressively hot conditions. My first and last match here ended in disaster with me being carried from the court with severe heat exhaustion. An ambulance arrived complete with saline drip to reverse my dehydration, and that was the end of that tournament. I had hydrated very well the night before. I had learnt from previous episodes. I was supremely fit and healthy, so why was this still happening?

Until I could find answers I simply had to play on and keep preparing the only way I knew how. One way or another, I was only a short few days from returning home to Australia. I had given this a very good shot. I had done my best and I was comfortable with that, however, deep down I knew I didn't get what I had been there for. I was now twenty-one years of age, and time was ticking, as always. Time stops for nothing or nobody. And with each day that passed, the 'making it' option was slipping further away.

***

I broke down as I relived the Wolters match in detail with my brothers when I arrived home.

'I had the guy on toast. And then in the blink of an eye... I ...I... choked. Big time.'

My eldest brother John, perhaps sensing my exasperation, gave me a hug and, almost like an intervention, said, 'Mate, how about Lisa and I take you down to the next tournament and watch?'

I gave him a watery smile. 'Thanks Johnno, that would actually be a welcome change up.'

I'm so glad he offered because I feel I really needed his support. I had been in the US for the previous eight weeks basically alone. No coach. No family. No real support, but for my Aussie mates. Even these blokes had their own fish to fry. In reality, I found it a lonely lifestyle and real challenge to the perception for many of life 'on the tour'. John had always looked out for me as my oldest brother, and being a very compassionate bloke, he could see the timing was right. The rest of my family were supportive too, but John was the right person for this moment.

As much as Dad had been a mainstay at tennis tournaments with me for so many years, I think he was happy to be relieved of this duty once I went to college. He had given up countless weekends for all four of us boys for so many years, as swimming coach, tennis coach, and in the role of sports parent chauffeur.

So, as if to whack me in the face with reality, I was sent to the furthest court at the Gold Coast tournament where my brother John watched me play my first-round match. It would turn out to be a life defining moment. I raced to a one set lead, before relinquishing the second set. Sound familiar?

As the third set approached, it hit me. I was on a back court on the Gold Coast in a tournament that meant nothing to me. I was not sure why I was even playing the event. It was not a good place to be emotionally. I competed my best which was automatic for me as I didn't know any other way. But it was the closest thing I had come to tanking. In reality, I had given myself no real chance to win the match simply because I was not focusing on each point. I was in the midst of what I refer to as an unconscious tank. My mind had far bigger things to contemplate, and this match was not one of them.

I have sometimes wondered what would have happened to my tennis career had I not played this event and had a break. But I am eternally grateful that I did play because it exposed me.

It exposed me for all of my vulnerability. Into the third set, my whole tennis life, the whole kit bag of good and bad experiences seemed to appear in front of me as if I was watching a slideshow. The early successes, followed by the expectations, the rushing, the uncertainty, the guilt of asking my parents to fund my expensive dream, nagging worry about my heart complaint rearing its head again; the recent heartbreak of choking and recurring stories of my body letting me down. All of it was there that day.

At some point in the journey, I'd forgotten what I played for. Enjoyment was the key to my success rather than success being the key to my enjoyment. And if enjoyment was the key, then why was I playing this entire final set through tears?

The realisation hit me like a Mack truck. I had been making decisions to please others; not one person in particular. It was the very first time I had realised why I played this game. I enjoyed it, I was good at it, but there was more to me than just tennis. I left the court, and John's demeanour was one of absolute pity and concern for his little brother. He hadn't seen me play for years but to see me like this wasn't the plan. In the car, I let it all out, and it felt absolutely liberating, if not a little embarrassing.

'I bloody hate tennis!' I sobbed.

John bent his arm awkwardly to pat my back from the driver's seat. 'No, you don't, mate. I just think you need a rest and you need some time at home, watching the footy, going to the movies like other people your age, and just taking your mind off things for a while.'

I leant forward to rest my head in my hands. 'But I can't afford to have time off. I've got to keep playing if I want to be any good.'

'But you *are* good. And why can't you just have two weeks off?' He gave my shoulder a shake.

'Because I'm running out of time to make it!'

John pulled the car over, eager to get his point across. 'Well mate, you aren't going to make it in this frame of mind. Sometimes you just need to take a step back and have a reset. The biggest question you need to ask yourself is, how do I get back to loving tennis?'

We arrived home and as normal, Mum asked, 'How'd you go love?'

'Not good,' I replied.

John, as if to protect me from going over everything we discussed in the car, took over from there and explained what had happened.

Sitting around the kitchen table, where all serious

discussions were held, Mum simply asked me two questions.

Two of those rhetorical questions that she had the knack of throwing out there at the right time. 'Do you ever sit back and think, that maybe this professional tennis thing might not be for you?' And, 'Do you think that the heart business, the heat exhaustion issues, the tight losses, and the fact that you love the team tennis in the US is telling you something?'

Prior to that day, my answer would have been emphatically, 'No Mum, I'm doing this.'

I had always loved stories of successful sports stars who had overcome adversities. They all had their moment of truth, doubt, and distress before overcoming them. I was to be one of them, I always thought.

Today though, Mum's questions, on the back of my emotional chat with John, got through to me. I didn't answer her questions, but, wiping tears away, I smiled at Mum sheepishly and headed for the refuge of my bedroom. I lay there, gazing at my walls covered by posters of Agassi, Cash, Rafter, Becker, and Edberg. There, I imagined my life without trying to become a professional tennis player. And the more I thought about it, the more it looked pretty rosy.

That day, I confronted the Wolters loss, the other heartbreaking losses, the heart issues, the chronic cramping, and became thankful for them. After all, they led me here to this very moment. It was the moment I became ok with it all. It was the moment I let go of the expectations of others and my own. It was the moment I became an adult, and I was about to make my first adult decision; one that would become the best of my life to that point.

10

AMERICA 3.0 – MAKING THINGS RIGHT

I could hardly wait to get back on the phone to Coach. 'Coach, I'm coming back again, will you take me?'

Coach laughed uncomfortably at first. 'Chris, I've heard all this before. You know we'd love to have you. But how can I trust that you are for real this time? Besides, your grades won't allow you to come here on scholarship.'

I took a deep breath and barrelled forward. 'I have promised my parents I will make this work and I will make the same promise to you. I will make this work. I will pay the difference myself. I will save my own money.'

I said it, I meant it, and I knew I would do it. Because I knew this is what I wanted, finally. Definitely.

This new-found clarity gave me a phenomenal amount of energy. I was going back to Oklahoma, my home away from home. This time, I knew why I was going. I was there to graduate, compete well, enjoy my experience, and start getting ready for life after tennis.

Nothing had changed in the town of Stillwater when I returned in time for the spring season. It was still cold and windy. Coach's jokes hadn't changed. Belt buckles, cowboy hats, and awkwardly tight jeans were still powerful statements of fashion. My tennis world *had* changed though.

Pavel and Martin, the two Czechs on the team, had graduated. Pavel, having won national collegiate titles in singles and doubles with Martin, had taken off back to Prague to begin his new life there. Martin had completed his tennis eligibility but still had some subjects to complete his education. The other Aussies, Rob and Dan, finished their tennis but were still on campus to graduate. Brad, my doubles partner, had become the assistant coach whilst starting his post graduate MBA.

In my time back in Australia, two young Aussies and two Kiwis had been recruited to fill the roster along with a new Czech player and a few young Americans. Me, well, I was ineligible to play this semester until I could show the University that I was committed to my studies. This was the directive from the NCAA based on my poor academic record from last semester. You see, the collegiate system in the USA is all about being a successful student-athlete. Student first. Athlete second. This was my price to pay and it was the best thing that had happened to me.

This semester was about getting into a routine of study and focus. It was also a chance to discover the value of money and saving. It was my money this time, so I was determined to make it work. I had been given a third chance and I was going to take it. I was not permitted to practice with the tennis team as part of the sanction, but I stuck to my own rigid training program.

That semester, I grew up. I attended every lecture with great vigour and interest. I could sense that those within the athletic department doubted my academic ability, and who could blame them based on my results that were there in black and white? I knew I was about to prove them wrong.

My first mission was to retake the classes I had failed last year which I did. One of these classes was American History. This time it was taught to me by a

Native American. His unique perspective intrigued me, and I asked a million questions of him over the course of that semester. His ability to delicately weave the issue of the plight of his people and the advancement of white colonisation throughout history without bias was inspirational. I received an A for the class. First mission accomplished.

Prior to my most recent departure from Stillwater, I took a consumer behaviour class that I found engaging. It was cool to learn what motivated humans to purchase. On the back of this class, my academic advisor enrolled me into some introductory economics and marketing subjects that semester to explore this field some more.

'Third time lucky, huh?' he asked. 'Let's make the most of this last chance. Time to take control of your future. You've shown interest in my stories about my small businesses. Why don't we try some new subjects?'

I thoroughly enjoyed learning about the real world, about people, about how the world goes around. Economics, finance, and business were all important subjects to know about, because if tennis wasn't going to be my number one focus, I was going to benefit from knowing this subject matter. So, I thoroughly immersed myself into all these subjects and my grades reflected my newfound interest. Maybe I could become a student after all!

The semester passed by so fast. I was missing tennis, but this academic focus was something that took me by complete surprise. I became an accidental student.

The lessons out of the classroom were profound too. My eyes were open; truly open. I began to notice things I had never seen before which were right in front of me. Just a short bike ride from my apartment, en route daily to campus, I passed a little old, white, run-down house. It looked like most other houses around campus. Except now, I was looking closely. This house seemed to have an inscription etched into the front wooden veneer above the entrance.

One day I squeezed the brakes on the bike and took closer inspection of the inscription.

Garth Brooks Lived Here, it read.

Well that's pretty cool, I thought. I imagined what circumstances led to Garth Brooks going from a college athlete in Oklahoma to one of the most successful country music stars on the planet.

When I jumped on the practice court or in the gym, I felt good. I felt like there was much more to me than tennis and therefore my tennis was not who I was; it was simply something that I did. I could enjoy the game, the discipline of training, and the thrill of competition. But there wasn't a nagging struggle hovering overhead about success versus failure.

The power of education had reared its head and it was as if my brain had been waiting for this opportunity all along. I just couldn't see it through the haze of fuzzy yellow tennis balls and tennis courts.

***

Lessons On Reflection:

I wonder how many athletes' performances are affected by what I call 'non-competition overheads' – those off-court, unseen pressures that impact the way one approaches competition.

For a junior tennis player in Australia, think about the pressures. In a match, there is scoreboard pressure. There are nerves to manage. These are all fair game and part of being a competitor. Great books and even better coaches can help players learn to manage these situations. But how do we trace the impact of the off-court pressures on any given match result?

Often the following factors are invisible and almost impossible to detect:

- *Pressure (direct or indirect) from family to perform,*
- *The worry of points chasing,*

- *The worry of ranking implications of winning and losing,*
- *A pending exam or assignment due the following week,*
- *An issue within a school friendship group as part of growing up.*

Parents and coaches need to first be aware of these factors and the fact that they play a huge role in performance on the weekend. The hard part is that they are unseen worries.

So, awareness is step one.

Step two is to normalise these worries and concerns with young athletes.

Step three is for parents and coaches to model positivity and the importance of focusing on the process rather than outcomes. Parents and coaches, myself included, can sometimes inadvertently model the same worries listed above which only serve to add pressure to the player.

For me, my biggest non-competition overhead was this nagging idea that success will be defined if I 'make it' and failure is if I don't. I took this subconsciously into every match I played for many years until that day on the Gold Coast when it was stripped bare. The irony here is that with the overhead removed, I was able to play the best tennis of my life from that point on, and I was comfortable *that my best tennis was going to be on college courts across the USA and not on the professional tour.*

In fact, at this juncture I was not tempted to play professionally. I was simply happy playing, maximising my ability, but with other more important newfound focuses.

***

As May approached, rather than preparing for another trip home, I was planning my summer school classes. I still had three more classes to regain my tennis eligibility for the start of the next semester. My summer classes were taken across six weeks and my eligibility was now intact. I still had another two years of tennis left to play and I was now back on track academically. The wrongs of the past year had been corrected. My failed classes had now been passed with flying colours. There was just one thing left to do – try to earn some money to pay back my parents.

My new South African roomie, Jacques, with flowing blonde locks and an enviable tan to boot, had transferred from another college to play at Oklahoma State. He had told me how fantastic his summer coaching opportunities had been in New York. He arranged for me to go with him to the Hamptons in New York for the last four weeks of summer to take part in summer camp coaching.

Nothing could have prepared me for what awaited. This was a whole new world – a world where the rich and famous commuted back and forth by helicopter from work in Manhattan to their holiday houses in the Hamptons. For a young Aussie this was the epitome of a land of opportunity.

The camp days were long with hundreds of pre-teen kids giggling and screaming with every strike of the ball. When the camp days were over, other coaches wanted to practice with me. Soon, parents and club members wanted to have some hitting sessions with a college tennis player. They were willing to pay for it too which was gleefully accepted.

After two weeks, I had shown a willingness to work hard from cleaning courts, cooking lunch on the BBQ for the masses, supervising the bus pick up and drop offs of the kids, to answering the front desk phone. The owner of the camps soon saw that he could entrust me with his most high-profile clients and before I knew it a whole new world opened to me.

One day I was asked to hit with a club member. He didn't want to be coached – he simply wanted to hit against a left-hander as he wanted to beat a colleague who was a lefty.

When he arrived, we shook hands, and wandered

to the court. I recognised him right away, and I resisted the temptation to ask for a photo and autograph. *Maybe after the session*, I thought.

'Ok, what would you like to work on, mate?'

'Just rallying today. Need to get used playing a lefty. I play with a lefty once a week for bragging rights.'

'No worries, I will try and show you what lefties don't like!'

With not much said for the rest of the session, that was that. I had just coached funny-man, Chevy Chase.

Later that day, I took a call from the Hilton family asking to coach their twin sons. When the lesson was over, older sister, Paris, arrived to pick them up and jumped on court for a session too. On another occasion a few days later, I was told that a seventeen-year-old player was looking to hit with a college player as he prepared to start his college career. When that session was over, his dad, my hero John McEnroe arrived to pick him up. I recall purposefully trying to showcase my best Johnny Mac volleys as he arrived. Unfortunately, I didn't get a chance to talk to him.

In another week, Rick Moranis, from *Honey I Shrunk the Kids* was another of my temporary pupils.

In the same week, Jimmy Buffet stopped by to say

thanks for coaching his son with tickets to watch his show that weekend, complete with backstage passes. After the show, some other coaches and I were greeted by a middle-aged roadie rocker who was the spitting image of Cher. Barb, as her name tag read, ushered us backstage where we briefly met the band. The conversation was short, but the memories were lasting. We were ushered back out as the crowd chanted, 'Encore! Encore! Encore!'

This was some week! At the time I did not know Jimmy Buffet's music too well, but after this particular evening I was transported to this wonderful place called Margaritaville, a song which still today features on our family Spotify playlist entitled, 'Essential Road Trip Songs'. He was a very generous and friendly man. By the way he interacted with the crowd and his fans, it wasn't hard to work out why he had such a huge following from the baby-boomer generation.

In between these once in a lifetime brushes with fame, I was housesitting mansions, handling family credit cards to use at will (not that I did!), doing house visits to coach families privately and getting paid handsomely. Lifelong friends were made with other coaches from all around the world.

Positive lessons were learnt; work hard, treat people right, provide good service and rewards will come. Indeed, the parents of the happy little campers at the conclusion of the summer delivered extremely generous cash tips to be divided among coaches. The steps were put in place to do it all again the following summer. I could only hope that the following summer would be equally as surreal.

***

Lessons On Reflection:

That summer, on the back of multiple economics and marketing classes, was my first experience witnessing the fact that consumers were willing to pay money for people and their services if they saw value and a solution in doing so. This was the power of education – both in the classroom and in real life action. The seed was planted in that consumer behaviour class.

I loved America's attitude to entrepreneurship. If a person or business entity was providing a good or service, American society was willing to pay for it without fuss or judgment.

Nobody told me about this before I went to college. I vowed to educate as many people as I could about these additional benefits of the college experience at any opportunity.

11

THE TEAM COMES FIRST

February 2000

'Dear Gram...

I'm absolutely loving going to Uni classes every day. My professors make it interesting and their open-door policy has been so good for me. If I ask for help, they give it to me happily because I think they can see I am working hard and am eager to learn, despite my results in the past.'

***

The next school year, my first full year, was simply a dream. My teammates were a different group of guys this time round. There was Matt and Marc, two Kiwis, big and small, respectively. Matt had a frame more built for rugby and a serve and forehand to match. He was a member of the New Zealand Davis Cup Team and had a certain air of confidence about him. Marc reminded me a lot of myself in my first semester. He was wide eyed, had a healthy sense of humour, found it easy to meet new friends, but I could also clearly see that he was taking some time to settle into cowboy country. Despite his very small stature (he made me look like a giant) he was a very solid player. I remember his first session and carefully watched his interactions with Coach.

Afterwards, I reassured him. 'Mate, don't take it personally if Coach tears your game apart.'

He gave me a confident thumbs up. 'Yeah, sweet-as. It will take me some time to get used to it. My coach back home was very quiet and super positive.'

I ruffled his hair, in the same manner Brad did mine back in my first session years earlier. 'I get it, mate. It's just another thing to get used to. But you will. Just hang in there.'

I would talk to him at the end of each session and kept an eye on him around campus. We took a political science class together and we would sit down for lunch most days. I suppose I was trying to ease his mind and help normalise his feelings as much as I could.

Matt on the other hand saw me initially as a rival

within the team. The feeling was mutual. Having missed a season and determined to repay Coach's faith in getting me back for a third time, I wanted to assert my authority. For the first few days I watched him at practice destroying my other teammates in point play. Then Coach put him up against me for the first time to play a set. It was that moment in the season that Coach liked to ramp things up, both in volume and intensity. Memories of my first few weeks of college came vividly bounding back to me.

In windy and cold conditions, I beat Matt 6-0 in the set, and remember an exchange between Matt and Coach bringing a smile to my face.

'What the hell am I supposed to do against this guy?' Matt bounced his racquet against the ground in frustration.

'Well, that's what you need to figure out, Matt. This is college tennis. You are going to come up against a lot of Batesy's who are crafty, know their own game, and know how to play to these conditions.'

That first set aside, I had earned Matt's respect and soon I could see that he was a heck of a strong player who was going to be the mainstay of this team for the next few years. Later on that season we would team up in doubles for a short period which proved to be successful.

There was Jiri the Czech, who, behind the look of a librarian had a lethal game from the back of the court. Frantisek, aka Frankie from Slovakia, was a warrior. Muscly and without any obvious signs of body fat, Frankie would rarely walk off court without blood and sweat oozing from a knee or elbow, such was his commitment to winning at all physical costs.

Coach planned one heck of an awesome travel schedule this year. Among many other exciting road trips, we travelled as a team to New Orleans, to California, and over to Harvard, where James Blake, a future top 10 ATP player played in the #1 position.

New Orleans was a memorable trip. By then we had spent a few months together, and my whole team was new. It was our first major trip away, and as a senior player, I thoroughly enjoyed getting to know the boys better and playing the role as leader on and off-court. It was also the time of year that Mardi Gras took place. The streets were lined with food, dancing music, colour, and misbehaviour. The photos from this trip are forever etched in the memory of a time which epitomises all that is great about this college experience; the travel, the camaraderie, the competition and now, later on, the memories.

I loved the idea of travelling with a team uniform

through airport after airport, staying in hotels, eating well when we won, and eating fast when we lost.

The highlight came one August night in Tulsa as we attempted to qualify for the National Team Indoor Championships. To qualify we needed to knock off University of Kansas, New Mexico, and Indiana State to make the sixteen-team national invitational.

Not as talented as the previous cowboy teams in which I had played, this team defied the odds to meet Indiana State for the chance to go to Nationals. It was a phenomenal achievement simply to qualify for this final match.

The match was an epic encounter. The umpires played a key role in ensuring the opposition kept their dubious line calls to a minimum which caused a great degree of consternation from the opposition coaches.

Cramps set in once again for me, but I was able to play myself through the discomfort to get a satisfying victory, even though in the end my match result was not required. Our team had lifted immensely, and we pulled off an incredibly gutsy win against a much more mature team. To this point, it was the most enjoyable college team victory I had been a part of because we all clicked and played our best tennis simultaneously. This is a rarity in team sport. Even better, we had just qualified for indoor nationals, something the previous team had not done.

We celebrated hard that night with loud, dodgy Czech music and a hybrid game of cricket, ice hockey, and baseball with anyone who wanted to play. The details are very sketchy but if you could imagine three rubbish bins as bases, around which the batter had to run to make it back to home plate. To hit the ball, the batter could opt for a hockey stick, cricket bat, or baseball bat. At each base there were food and drink stations to add to the craziness.

Thankfully, we had an endless supply of tennis balls to use as dozens were dispatched onto the roofs and into the backyards of an unsuspecting Stillwater street. It was one of those rare great team moments where we could all sit back and admire each other's efforts that day.

Later that semester, at the Indoor National Championships held at the beautiful University of Washington campus in Seattle, we drew the number one seed, The University of Tennessee in the first round.

By this stage we were gelling as a team, and I was thoroughly enjoying my role as a leader on the team. I felt like a coach rather than just a player. In truth, my experiences had helped me help these other youngsters. I saw some of me in them and could easily help them on and off-court. I was always looking for the right words to inspire the younger guys to be ready to play their hearts out. I didn't have to look too far for inspiration.

The night before the match against Tennessee, I entered a lift after the opening banquet, only to be greeted by the entire Tennessee team, many of whom were Australians.

'G'day boys,' I said as I began to recognise them all one-by-one.

Crickets. Dead silence. *Ok, ok,* I thought. *I see what's going on here. Getting serious about the big match tomorrow, eh?*

So, I decided to make the elevator ride uncomfortable for everybody, simply by making eye contact. The next time you get in a lift with a stranger take the time to notice what happens when the door closes. Humans will look down or up, never straight ahead, and never facing one another. So, I decided to make eye contact with every single person in that lift. It was *very* uncomfortable. I relayed this moment with the team the following morning at breakfast.

I beckoned the team to lean in. 'Boys gather around. I've got something to share.'

Matt joked, 'What, are Tennessee forfeiting the match today?'

'No, it's better than that. Listen up.' I told them the story, embellishing the fact that these guys thought we were not worthy of being here at this tournament.

'How do you feel about that, Jiri? Frankie?

The pep talk had the desired effect. I had never seen their eyes so steely, so focused. We were all pumped and angry. We were ready for battle.

History shows that, just four hours later, our 45th ranked Cowboys knocked off the Tennessee Vols, the number one seed in the tournament, the number two ranked team in the Division 1 NCAA competition in the USA. It was a super moment, immensely gratifying, especially given the antics the night before of our opponents. To this day, it is the biggest boilover victory in the history of the NCAA Division 1 indoor national titles.

Personally, my win against more highly fancied opponent, Mario Toledo, was my most satisfying of my entire college career. The huge win put our team into the top twenty ranked programs in the USA, my singles ranking into the top hundred rankings in the whole of the US for the first time, and later, when the doubles rankings were updated, Frankie and I were judged to be in the top fifteen ranked doubles pairings nationwide.

This represented the best week of my life at college to that point, and it felt that all of the wins and losses prior led to this moment. It also showed me that if my focus was not on myself, as was the nature of an individual sport, it brought the best out in me and in my teammates.

Perhaps I am destined to be a better teacher or coach than a player, I pondered that night as I went through my normal bedtime post-match post-mortem.

As if the trip could not get any better, earlier that night Coach received a message from Desmond Mason, former Cowboys basketball sensation, now key player for the Seattle Sonics in the NBA. Mason had seen the story of our win on the Seattle news and invited us to watch him play the next night. At one point 'D-Mase' motioned to us in the crowd (it wasn't hard for us to stand out in bright orange against a sea of green) in the midst of dunking.

What a moment!

We were jumping up and down like school kids. We couldn't have scripted this any better.

'He actually pointed at us; did you guys see that?'

'How good is this, Batesy!' Frankie screamed back.

After the game we were treated to dressing room passes to meet the entire team including legends,

Gary Payton and Patrick Ewing. A bigger human I had never seen. In years to come, Des Mason would win back to back NBA Slam Dunk contests.

Years earlier, I had come to know and really like him as a guy. Des was an artist, and we enjoyed taking an art class elective together, which he would later choose as his major. He still produces some amazing art to this day in his retirement from basketball and although nowhere near Des's ability, creating art remains one of my favourite switch-off hobbies.

At season's end I was able to pay for my own trip home with the money I had saved. I cherished these precious weeks over Christmas, the most magical time of the year. It was noted by those that knew me well how much more relaxed I had seemed that Christmas.

My observation of my parents was similar. They seemed very content and perhaps relieved that I had found my path and discovered my true purpose. The transformation was obvious when I spent more time that Christmas talking about my subjects of choice and the academic awards I had achieved for that year than any sporting moments.

***

Lessons On Reflection:
It was any wonder I was talking about my academic

achievements that Christmas. Never before had I received any academic recognition like I did in the US. The US collegiate system recognises that student-athletes have much to juggle; more so than a non-athlete. If a student-athlete can achieve a certain GPA (grade point average) they will value it, recognise it, celebrate it, and reward it. If somebody is doing a good job, the American way is to tell him or her. That's what I like about the culture in the US.

I had nudged my GPA to just under an A average through hard work and commitment and it was acknowledged in the local paper, The Daily O' Collegian, and with a certificate to add to the resume. They even had 'All-Academic' teams within our conference to recognise the players in the competition with the best GPA's. Always focused on academic achievement. This was and is a hallmark of the US college culture; vastly different to anywhere else in the world.

Those that improved their GPA's were also recognised at special student-athlete academic banquets. It's not just about rewarding the best of the best. The implicit message here is that academics matter, improvement matters, and it all deserves to be celebrated. Our education system in Australia could learn a lot from this.

12

SAVOURING THE ON - COURT MOMENTS

May 2000

"Dear Gram,

The more I think of my last few years, this whole college idea is really a no-brainer. I could write a book about it. In fact, I will Grammy; I promise I will write that book..."

***

My final year of tennis was hectic but exceptionally transformative. The previous year I had lived my 'this is what I need to be doing' moment. My final year was about relishing my final season and preparing for life after college. Despite being my last year of playing eligibility, it was also a year of many firsts. We were lucky enough to travel via private Oklahoma State University aircraft to one match in College Station, Texas, taking off from the Stillwater 'international' airport. The ten-seater pulled up just metres from the courts, where, waiting for us was the deafening sound of the Texas A&M fight song, on repeat, blaring out over the courts as we warmed up. This lasted an hour.

If that wasn't intimidating enough, just prior to the national anthem before the match, a teammate pointed out President George Bush Sr standing in the crowd. We were mesmerised by the happenings around us, and when our opponents were literally doing cartwheels after breaking my serve in the first doubles, the circus was complete. Who knew that there could really be such thing as a home-ground advantage in tennis?

That season, on-court we beat those we were expected to and conversely, lost to those we expected would beat us. An exception came indoors at the University of Arkansas against the highly ranked, Razorbacks. Playing with Frankie in doubles we continued to win the majority of our doubles and the Kiwi doubles combo of Matt and Eru helped us get off to a great start by winning the doubles point for the team. This dual match followed that trend. It would be my last ever match indoors, and one that I felt I was in control of right from the warmup.

If I could have bottled that sort of confidence and focus, I could have sold it for a small fortune. It remains the great mystery across sport as to why it is near impossible to stay 'in the zone' for competition after competition.

The win over Arkansas put us firmly inside the top forty and another NCAA Championship berth was inevitable as we approached the month of May.

As I sat back after my singles win to cheer on my teammates that night against Arkansas, I became quite nostalgic about my college experience. I reflected on the unique and often tribal structure of college tennis in the sense that all six singles matches were played at once.

This made for such an exciting dynamic. If you look at any given individual tournament where there is a row of six matches side by side, each player is battling their own battle and their own opponent. It's a private, lonely battle. In college, with scoreboards ticking over on each court, you can see how your teammates are going. Go to a college match and you will hear the player on court one screaming encouragement across to court six, and everywhere in between. As a participant, it lifts you.

It takes some getting used to, but ultimately it makes for an exhilarating team atmosphere. Yes, I wanted to win my match. But I wanted to win for my team; my brothers.

In college, team is family. Each player, Americans included, are living away from home so each team member is experiencing the highs and lows of life without their normal support mechanisms. Team really does become family. When we won, we won together and celebrated. When we lost, we lost together and supported one another.

Over four years, a college player will invariably be placed in the situation where he or she will be last match on with scores level. It will come down to that match. I have come to believe that you haven't fully experienced the joys of college tennis until faced with this situation. In that last year, I had my moment against the University of Tulsa, a strong Oklahoma rival.

It was a typically mild yet windy April afternoon and as the sun headed west to rest up for the next day, we were closing in on victory. A quick glance across all courts showed we were in a tight match but leading on most courts. In an instant, momentum shifted as one match turned Tulsa's way and the loud positive outburst of emotion from the Tulsa player seemed to permeate across all other courts.

Having lost a rare doubles point, we needed to win four of the six singles ties. With each cheer of the Tulsa crowd, pressure built, and I could sense from Coach's pacing and increasingly worried facial expression that we were in trouble.

As each match finished, the crowd moved to the next 'swing match' much like the infamous Cal Berkeley a few seasons earlier. On this day, my final home-game as a Cowboy, that swing match was again my match. My Polish opponent was ranked inside the top 100 in the US, as was I at this point, but his recent results were super impressive.

Coach stayed well away from my court, perhaps knowing that I found his nerves to be contagious. My old mate Brad, now assistant coach, gave me a few Aussie-style pep talks during the final set and it did the trick. I was very focussed although at one change of ends I caught a glimpse in the stands of all of the wonderful people that I had met over my four years in college. Some had driven hours to watch my last match. I was fired up to win this one.

The next fifteen minutes my opponent tightened right up, understandably, and I was thankful to be on the winning side of such a tight match for a change. My college career started with some heartbreaking losses and my last home game finished on such a high. I was a better player now; a much smarter player. Importantly, I was a happy player just playing, just like when I was twelve years old.

That night, the famous Eskimo Joes, chilli cheese fries never tasted so good.

After conference championships, which ended in the semi-finals, Coach gave us the news that we had been drawn to play our first two rounds of Nationals at the famed stadium at Stanford University. We were headed for California where we would play the University of Florida in the first round of the sixty-four-team tournament with a chance to play Stanford in the round of thirty-two.

Nothing could have prepared me for what I experienced on the hallowed courts of Stanford – the place graced by the likes of Roscoe Tanner, John McEnroe my hero, and so many other eventual professionals. Indeed, as we sat in the player's lounge before the match against Florida, we were surrounded by an overflowing trophy cabinet adorned with memorabilia of winning and success every way we turned. We were in the presence of proven winners. First, we had to get past Florida in order to get a shot at Stanford.

The team did just that. We beat Florida and beat them well. I played one of my better matches that season with legendary Stanford coach, Dick Gould, watching on. We'd made it through to the next round against Stanford who had a comfortable victory of their own.

I woke up very stiff and sore for the Stanford match and tried all I could to stretch it out and sweat it out in the warmup. I felt good heading into the doubles and in the number one position, Frankie and I battled hard against future ATP top one-hundred player Alex Kim and his partner. We weren't quite good enough and we lost the team doubles point.

Now, for potentially my final ever collegiate match.

I was pitted against KJ Hippensteel. I had seen him play the previous day and I was impressed by his 'leftiness' (in truth I hated playing fellow lefties) and his versatility. I overheard Coach Gould warning KJ about my ability to play the conditions well and to fight hard for every point. I liked hearing that.

Apparently KJ didn't need to hear it because from the very first point he was fearless and on fire. At no stage in this match did I feel 'in it' – in fact, I was powerless and helpless to his power and precision. It was only against him and my old roomie, Pavel, did I ever feel helpless on a court. Against all others, I always felt like I was a chance. At the net, I remember shaking hands with KJ thinking, *I'm going* to remember this guy's name – he's got what it takes to make it.

It felt good to appraise other players and not worry about whether I was going to make it. Perhaps it was fitting that my college journey was book-ended by playing the best two of my opponents in my life; the great Pavel in that first training session, and KJ Hippensteel in my last.

I also remember soaking in a great atmosphere. This was a stadium court and there were at least a few hundred paying fans watching, all adorned in cardinal red watching their beloved Stanford do their thing – win. I remember Coach Gould coming to shake my hand and congratulating me on a great college career. He also told me he had been looking forward to the Bates v Hippensteel match as he enjoyed our styles.

We were soundly beaten overall but on all courts we were more than competitive. At twilight, it was my last official team dinner, and Coach gave me the honour of asking me to choose a place to spend it together. It would be a fancy pizza joint. It was always disappointing to lose, of course, but on reflection that afternoon as the California sun disappeared, we were able to put our efforts in perspective over a few pepperoni and meat lover's pizzas.

Whilst Stanford and many other teams for that matter, trained year-round outdoors we had to travel indoors daily during the main season. Our facilities were sub-standard, but we never complained. Our success was based on good recruiting of doubles players, good competitors, and strong team unity built on those bus trips up and down highway I-35 daily to practice. We were all international players so we could all support each other – we were all in the same boat.

Hours after the pizza was inhaled, there I was, on a plane headed back to Oklahoma City, a very tired yet content young man. My last time officially in the orange and black travelling colours as a student–athlete. I would never get this opportunity again. Swept up in the moment and too overtired to sleep, I wrote to Grandma on the plane:

"*Grandma, the more I think about it, the more I feel like I want to write a book about my time in America. There is so much to tell and share with others about this amazing opportunity. It has actually been phenomenal.*"

I had exhausted all of my tennis eligibility, but I still had one summer of study in Stillwater, another Hamptons experience, a brother's wedding to attend back home, and one more semester of college classes to go before I was a graduate. It had worked out beautifully for me that this last seven months in the

US allowed for all of my lessons to sink in. It allowed time to prepare for the next phase of my life and it allowed me to save money for something very special.

I diarised a goal when I set upon USA 3.0. I wanted to give something back to my parents after all of their years of support and sacrifice. They were not privy to this goal, nor were they comfortable with the notion that I would pay for their air tickets to come to my graduation. But I insisted. It made me feel really proud that I was able to do it, but even more, just so happy to be able to say thank you in this way.

That last semester, I received such amazing support from Oklahoma State University. As a former student-athlete I remained on scholarship. I was able to access free resume assistance and mock interview preparation. The goal here was to find work in a marketing role in the USA and take advantage of a one-year visa that was afforded international students upon graduation – provided no crimes were committed as a foreign student. I was thankfully safe in this area and my new visa was granted.

Not surprisingly, my grades in my last semester were reflective of the enjoyment and settled attitude with which I approached studies. My academic advisor announced to me that I was now the newest member of the Business College's *Dean's List of Distinguished Students*. To this day that was my proudest achievement as a player or student.

Before too long, I was picking up Mum and Dad from Dallas airport ahead of my graduation.

Graduation day was a blur for me and quite overwhelming for Mum and Dad. They met what seemed like the entire university. Among them, the athletics staff who had put up with me for four years. My awesome teammates. My non-tennis friends. Families like the Horn family and Houk family, who had gone way above and beyond in their support for me and for the team.

Two famous scenes that I had seen in the movies of US college graduations were an inspiring speech from a successful person, and the group mortar board toss into the air. I was looking forward to both. However, I only remember the tossing of the mortar board, which was as cool as I had imagined. I cannot remember a word of the speech.

Truthfully, I was daydreaming.

Reliving moments. Moments in that very same building. Moments like some four years earlier witnessing college basketball in all its glory in my first semester as an Oklahoma State Cowboy. Moments like standing outside in the student-athlete section waiting for gates to open for a big basketball or wrestling match, singing 'Getting Jiggy With It' with my fellow cowboy and cowgirl athletes. Moments like seeing Superman, aka Christopher Reeve, inspiring students with his story of survival and contentment. Moments like speaking to thousands of young high school students as part of Open Day, highlighted by Desmond Mason asking me to be his springboard as he dunked over the top of me to the rapturous approval of pimply-faced kids.

The moment in this very arena in the very spot that I was seated, when twelve thousand deliriously happy fans broke the sound barrier smashing several lights in the process as an Oklahoma State wrestler won his bout against our instate rival Oklahoma University. Moment after moment, time after time when, descending the bleachers after another cowboys victory, mums, dads, grandparents and students alike would sing Toby Keith's 'Shoulda Been a Cowboy' and how that made me feel part of something bigger and special.

Boy, I was going to miss this place. One thing I was sure of though; I was always going to be a Cowboy. I felt valued there and it felt part of me.

Years later, as my wife entered this arena with me

for the first time, she was struck by the size, the sounds, and the passion which brought her to tears.

During that trip with my wife, at a break in proceedings between wrestling bouts between, you guessed it, Oklahoma State University and Oklahoma University, the announcer asked fans to turn their attention to the 'jumbotron' – a three-dimensional big screen located centrally right above the wrestling mat.

The lights dimmed and then the announcer said, 'Ladies and gentlemen, today in beautiful Stillwater we welcome back some very special Cowboys.'

The spotlight shone on two very identifiable athletes, sitting close by to each other.

'On break from the PGA Golf Tour, please give a cowboy welcome to Charles Howell the third! And ladies and gentlemen, the man to his right needs no Cowboy introduction – please welcome the one, the only, Barry Sanders!'

Sanders was one of the greatest American football players of all time.

As I leant in to explain to my wife who these famous cowboys were, we were blinded by the spotlight ourselves.

'And now, all the way from Brisbane, Australia, former Cowboy tennis star, Chris Bates!'

My wife was in tears again, I think really just

overwhelmed by how wonderful this community was. She was seeing for herself why I spoke with such passion about this part of my life. And, sure enough, as we exited the bleachers, proudly sung 'Shoulda Been a Cowboy' together.

But back to the graduation. After the graduation formalities and wedding-day-like photo frenzy, I gathered Mum and Dad and we made our way to Eskimo Joes. There could not have been a more fitting location for dinner on my final night as a student.

Fittingly, as we made our way from the Gallagher Iba Arena graduation ceremony to the icy steps of Eskimo Joes, there waiting for us was a huge gathering of more wonderful people; wonderful 'Okey' people who had been a big part of the reason I kept coming back. Awkwardly generous gifts were presented to me, none more overwhelming than the scrap book that had been handed to me with four years of paper clippings, photos, and priceless memories.

Dad, never too far away from getting emotional, lost it. Mum followed. Then me. It was all too much. I had been talking to Mum and Dad every week for the past four years about these magnificent people. After all, I had been taken in as their own at times over the past few years. So, for Mum and Dad to witness the warmth of these people firsthand I think made them realise just how special my life in Stillwater had been. As parents I could see their pride and relief that I had made the right decisions and they had supported these decisions.

Much the same as I was overcome a few years earlier down at the lonely tennis tournament on the Gold Coast, this was a moment to be savoured and proud of. Nothing else mattered than the fact I had achieved something pretty darn cool – I was a graduate of Oklahoma State University, and I was proudly lapping up my cap and gown moment.

I loved the moment, just days later, when Mum and Dad witnessed their first Oklahoma snow gently accumulating on the red brick Georgian-style architecture across campus. Only days later, we were all together when I received the call from Feist Publications in Oklahoma City that I had been successful in my first ever job interview. I was to be a sales associate in a highly successful family run company, starting in January.

But first, I was heading home to enjoy a summer of sand, surf, and family before starting the next chapter.

13

A FINAL COLLEGE REFLECTION

It hit me as the Qantas airbus burst through the last clouds and the smoky haze of Brisbane city came into view. I was feeling suitably good about myself and what I had just achieved. In essence, I went to college a boy, and came back a man. I went to college uncertain about my future and came back confident of taking on anything.

I went as a budding tennis pro with a chip on his shoulder and finished a thoroughly content and accomplished player. I went as a disinterested learner and came back on the *Dean's List of Distinguished Students*.

I had met lifelong friends from several different

countries. Travelled to all parts of the USA (some thirty plus states in fact). Laughed. Cried. Cramped. Choked. Won a lot. Lost a lot. Made so many mistakes. Learnt from all of them. Learnt so, so much about myself, others, the world around me, and how to make decisions. Above all, I was ready for anything and everything that may come my way.

At some stage, I knew that I was going to impart these learnings onto others so that they too might experience this precious opportunity.

14

MAY 2017

I'm sitting in my office in Brisbane writing. I'm writing this book; I'm up to a part you would have read. That part in my first semester in Oklahoma, playing that fateful match against the University of Texas for the conference championships. That dreaded loss to the mercurial, Nick Crowell. The phone rings. It's an Oklahoma number with the all too familiar 405 area code.

"Hello, Chris speaking."

"Chris, Nick Crowell here from Oklahoma University."

It took a long pause to pull together the pieces.

'No way, Nick! What a blast from the past – this is not happening!'

We exchanged pleasantries for some time before telling him that he has called me almost exactly twenty years to the day since we had played each other. We hadn't seen other since, nor had we spoken. Not only that, I shared the uncanny fact that I was writing a book about my college days and at the precise point in time that the phone rang, I was documenting that fateful moment when we played each other all those years ago.

I was actually stuck on the specifics as to how that match panned out – the types of details that I had been trying to forget, yet now that I was being honest with all of you, wanted to share openly and accurately. After all, despite the loss, the match was both momentous and formative, and deserved to have a place in the book. Nick was happy to fill the gaps to the point of knowing exactly what shots took place, and by whom, and how the match unfolded, point by excruciating point.

'How in the world do you remember this in such detail?' I asked him.

He laughed. 'I cannot tell you how many times I have relived that match both in my head and to all of my players I have coached. It was by far the best moment of my tennis career and the most memorable. It was the defining moment of my college career.'

'Well, I'm glad I could be part of your favourite moment, mate.'

'That's the thing about sport though isn't it –

those types of matches are what it's all about. Think about what we both learnt from that match – how to hang in there, pride in defeat, humility in winning. Win or lose, those moments are fun, and we cannot call ourselves true competitors until we have given our all, and won, and given our all, and lost. I had some heartbreakers later in my career, believe me. And I'm sure you had your fair share of winning moments. It's about learning from all of them and storing them to draw upon in later life.'

Now a successful college tennis coach, Nick was actually calling to discuss some potential players in Australia for recruiting purposes. But the timing of the call appeared to be linked with fate.

Curious, I asked, 'So... how did the rest of your playing career pan out?'

He sighed. 'I loved college so much, but I struggled my way through with a heart condition that really impacted my energy levels and my focus.'

Now this symmetry was getting spooky!

We talked, and talked, and obviously shared our 'matters of the heart' and all of a sudden it became apparent for both of us – we were now doing what we were meant to be doing. Our collective prior experiences, good, bad, and ugly at times, had led us here – to roles in coaching, mentoring, and education. Our phone conversation proved that this was far more than coincidence – it had to be.

Author's Note

I love writing. It was my favourite part of school and it is probably no surprise to me that I have ended up writing what I hope is the first of several books.

The more I wrote, the deeper I delved, and the more I found. Some of it was confronting for me, and some, I had subconsciously parked somewhere into the back of my mental garage.

A huge part of my journey just happened to include the trials and tribulations of the sport of tennis. But I would hope that those who do read this book whether it be friends, younger (or older) sportspeople, coaches, or sporting parents (not just from tennis) will find it interesting, amusing, and perhaps find the inspiration to document their own journey.

Given my background over the past decade or so in teaching, coaching, and mentoring, occasionally throughout the book I couldn't resist putting my coaching and teaching hat on, touching on some of the lessons I'd learnt along the way that may be of use to readers.

Half-way through writing this book, I discovered some old letters that I had collected from my Grandma's house after she had passed away. These were letters we had exchanged throughout my US college years. Grandma was my biggest supporter and was just one of those types of positive, happy, and funny people you miss when not in her company. She was the first person I would visit when I won a trophy as a kid, the last person I'd say goodbye to before I left each time to the US, and my first stop-over directly from the airport to visit whenever I returned home. This was why I included snippets from those letters throughout the book. The very last letter I wrote to Grandma included a promise that I would write a book one day about my time in college. This book makes true that promise.

Acknowledgments

It goes without saying that nothing I have experienced in life has been possible without Mum and Dad. But it should not go without saying that there is no way I would have had the guts or wisdom to make the choices I have made without their guidance and support.

To my big brothers – thanks for keeping me grounded and lifting me up when needed. Thanks for being as stupidly passionate about life and sport as I am. It ensures that family barbecues will never be dull.

To all the coaches over the years who have in their own way shaped my game on-court and my approach off-court. My uncle, Max Bates, Ray Kelly, Milton Rothman, Wayne Hampson, Coach Wadley, and of course Dad – you've all had a positive impact in different ways.

My enjoyment in tennis came from my mates who often doubled as fierce rivals – Tony Burns, Simon Merrin, Jimmy Rapkins, Paul Hanley, Jay Gooding, and Anthony Ross immediately come to mind. I've been lucky enough to continue to work professionally with Anthony years beyond our last competitive match and with whom I've shared a passion for developing good players and good humans.

To my college teammates, my other brothers – in particular Rob Howarth, Daniel Russo, Pavel Kudrnac, Martin Dvoracek, and my doubles partners: Matt Prentice, Frankie Krepelka, and my great mate, Brad Chiller. My gratitude to you for sharing in this phenomenal once-in-a-lifetime experience we call college tennis. I hope that this book does it justice.

My heartfelt thanks to the Horn family, the Spearman's, the Houk's, Allison's and Ninman's – my adopted American families. What a great advertisement you are for down-to-earth good ol' American hospitality – you are the reason that Oklahoma is my second home.

To America – thank you! What a great country

and what a powerful and elaborate system you have created in collegiate sport! Thank you for including us foreigners and allowing us to share in your culture and experience what I have come to believe is the greatest opportunity for young sportspeople in the world. And thanks Oklahoma State University for shaping me for four spectacular years – my choice to become a Cowboy really was a 'game changer'.

In my first year in college, renowned Australian poet Rupert McCall took the time to mail me his books of poetry to keep me connected to home via rhyme and verse. My gratitude to you Rupert and thank you for allowing my favourite line from one of your poems to grace the pages in this book.

To Emily Craven – author and editor extraordinaire – your patience and ability to eke more and more detail out of my story I am truly thankful for. I can't be sure this project would have ever been completed without your input.

Last, and most importantly, a huge hug and kiss to my gorgeous wife, Alexia. Although I met you well after my last college days, you and our son Sidney are further inspiration for me to write and share my story. Thank you for believing in me and listening to my incessant ideas over the breakfast table. I love you both to Stillwater and back!

About the Author

Chris Bates is a coach, mentor, teacher, and founder of Study & Play USA, a family-run organization that facilitates the entire process for student-athletes right around the world to find their right-fit University opportunity in the US college system.

After winning several state and national tennis titles across Australia as a junior, it was fate, he believes, that lead him to Oklahoma State University to take up his own study and play opportunity. Four years later, having become a top one-hundred ranked Division 1 singles player, and top fifteen ranked doubles player, he graduated with a Bachelor of Business in Marketing, worked in Marketing roles in the USA briefly, before returning to his hometown in Australia.

Having coached multiple individual state and national tennis champions, Chris achieved success coaching Brisbane Boys' College several times to state team titles and a national title. This ignited a passion for mentoring youngsters which led to a brief teaching career where Chris taught English and Commerce at secondary school level. Study & Play USA eventually pried him away from his teaching career, however, his ability to maintain his role as a mentor within this capacity as Director provides him much gratification. Above all, his greatest joy is reserved for his son, Sidney, his wife, Alexia, and his wider family.

www.ingramcontent.com/pod-product-compliance
Lightning Source LLC
Chambersburg PA
CBHW030254010526
44107CB00053B/1703